JIM ABBOTT

BY JOHN ROLFE

A *SPORTS ILLUSTRATED FOR KIDS* BOOK

Written by John Rolfe
Cover photograph by V.J. Lovero
Cover design by Pegi Goodman
Interior line art by Jane Davila
Produced by Angel Entertainment, Inc.

SPORTS ILLUSTRATED FOR KIDS is a trademark of THE TIME INC. MAGAZINE COMPANY

SPORTS ILLUSTRATED FOR KIDS Books is a joint imprint of Little, Brown and Company and Warner Juvenile Books.

Printed in the United States of America

First Printing: March 1991
10 9 8 7 6 5 4 3 2 1

Published simultaneously in Canada by Little, Brown & Company (Canada) Limited

Library of Congress Cataloging-in-Publication Data

Rolfe, John
   Jim Abbott / John Rolfe.
     p.   cm.
   "A Sports illustrated for kids book."
   Summary: A biography of the one-handed pitcher of the California Angels baseball team.
   ISBN 0-316-75459-5 (pbk.)
   1. Abbott, Jim, 1967-   —Juvenile literature. 2. Pitchers (Baseball) — United States — Biography — Juvenile Literature. 3. Baseball players — United States — Biography — Juvenile Literature.
   [1. Abbott, Jim, 1967-   . 2. Baseball players. 3. Physically handicapped.] I. Title.
   GV865.A26R65 1991
   [92]—dc20   90-55741
                                                                    CIP
                                                                    AC

This book is available in hardcover library binding from: Lerner Publications Company, 241 First Avenue North, Minneapolis, Minnesota 55401
1-800-328-4929
ISBN: 0-8225-3108-9

Contents

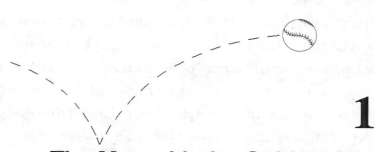

1
The Man with the Golden Arm

During the summer of 1988, a team of college baseball players from the United States traveled thousands of miles to fulfill a dream.

From June to September, Team USA played a total of 53 games in countries such as Italy and Japan. The players were often tired and homesick during the long journey. But when they took the field in Seoul, South Korea, on September 28, 1988, they were on the verge of having their dream come true. If they could beat Japan, they would become the first baseball team from the U.S. ever to win an Olympic gold medal!

Team USA placed its hopes that day on the arm of a

6'3", 205-pound, left-handed pitcher named Jim Abbott. Jim was the perfect choice to pitch the big game. Not only was he one of Team USA's best pitchers, he had also made a long and special journey of his own to acceptance as a player in the top ranks of amateur baseball. Because Jim Abbott was born without a right hand, he had to prove every step of the way that he was not limited by his handicap.

Jim had been amazing people with his skill as a baseball player ever since he was a little kid. At age 6, he taught himself to balance a baseball glove on the end of his right arm, throw the ball, and then slide his left hand into the glove so that he could catch the ball when it was hit or thrown to him. He still does this today. After Jim catches the ball, he cradles the glove in the crook of his right arm. Then he pulls his hand out, grabs the ball, and throws it.

Jim became so good at doing all those things quickly and smoothly that he was able to join a Little League team when he was 11 years old. He later became a star player in high school and even played quarterback on the varsity football team! At the University of Michigan, Jim was named America's top amateur baseball player and top amateur athlete in 1987. In 1988, he was chosen to play for

Team USA in the Summer Olympics.

By the time Jim arrived in Seoul, people all over the world had heard about him and they were fascinated by him. Fans and reporters from many different countries kept asking him how a person with one hand could ever become good enough to play baseball in the Olympics.

"I grew up learning to do things the way I am, with my capabilities, just the way anyone else learned to play ball with theirs," Jim explained. "I never really thought much about what it would have been like to be able to do it like everyone else."

There was a lot of pressure on Jim after he was chosen to pitch against Japan. The United States had not won a gold medal in baseball at a major international tournament such as the Olympics, the Pan Am Games, or the World Championships in 14 years. The U.S. baseball team had also lost to Japan in the gold medal game at the 1984 Olympics. Many Americans wanted Jim and his teammates to avenge that loss.

That day in Chamshil Baseball Stadium in Seoul, Jim overcame the pressure and made the world cheer for him. He allowed only one run in the first five innings as Team

USA took a 4-1 lead. In the sixth inning, Jim gave up two hits and walked a batter with the bases loaded. The score was soon 4-3. Mark Marquess, the head coach of Team USA, thought about bringing in a relief pitcher, but Jim settled down and pitched his way out of the jam. Twenty-four of Jim's next 28 pitches were strikes and he retired 11 of the last 12 batters he faced.

In the eighth inning, Jim made a play that snuffed out a rally that might have allowed Japan to tie the score. After the leadoff hitter singled, the next batter hit a sharp grounder right back at Jim. "I'd just got the glove back on my left hand when the ball arrived," he says. "I was thinking I could get a double play, but then, frankly, I just missed it."

The ball bounced off Jim's glove and rolled 20 feet away. He pounced on the ball and threw off-balance to first. The runner was out and the crowd went wild! Instead of having two runners on base, Japan now had only one. Jim retired the next two batters on ground balls and the inning was over.

"I thought the big defensive play of the game, both for Abbott and for the team, was the way he handled that comebacker in the eighth inning," Coach Marquess said.

Finally, with two outs in the ninth inning, Jim threw the biggest pitch of his life. The Japanese batter swung and hit a ground ball to third baseman Robin Ventura. First baseman Tino Martinez caught Ventura's throw for the final out and ran to the pitcher's mound. Martinez jumped into Jim's arms and they were soon buried under a pile of wildly happy teammates. The United States had won the gold medal!

"I never planned on being here, but I always sort of hoped for it," Jim told reporters. "This was my dream of a lifetime."

Six months later, another one of Jim's dreams came true. He began his career as a major league pitcher and won 12 games for the California Angels during the 1989 season. Jim Abbott is now one of the most promising young pitchers in the major leagues. His record for the 1990 season was 10-14 with a 4.51 ERA.

Jim is also one of the most remarkable players in baseball history. Many physically handicapped athletes have played in the major leagues, but very few were good enough to play for more than a few games or seasons.

One of the most famous handicapped major leaguers

was outfielder Pete Gray, who lost his right arm in an accident when he was 6 years old. Gray later played 77 games for the St. Louis Browns in 1945. The most successful player with a physical limitation was right-hander Mordecai Brown, who pitched for several major league teams from 1901 to 1920. Brown lost two fingers on his throwing hand in an accident when he was 7 years old. He was still able to throw a baseball and he later won 201 games during his major league career. Brown was elected to the Baseball Hall of Fame in 1949.

At first, many major league scouts and coaches doubted that Jim would be able to play in the big leagues. They did not think that he would be able to field bunts or catch balls that were hit hard right back at him. Jim proved that he could during his first season with the Angels. He is now expected to have a long, successful career.

"All the questions about Jim have pretty much been put aside," says Marcel Lachemann [*LATCH-man*], the Angels pitching coach. "Most important, he has proved that he has quality major league stuff — a great breaking ball, pitches inside to right handers, and he seems to throw his best pitches when he's in jams."

A pitcher who performs at his best when he's in a jam has "poise." Jim has had poise all his life. For example:

• When people doubted that Jim could play Little League baseball because of his handicap, he threw a no-hitter in the first game he pitched!

• When people doubted that Jim would be good enough to play baseball in high school, he made the varsity team in his sophomore year at Flint Central High School in Flint, Michigan. As a senior, Jim pitched 4 no-hitters and batted .472 with 7 home runs and 31 runs batted in!

• When people doubted that Jim would be good enough to play baseball in college, he won 26 games and lost only 8 during three years at the University of Michigan. In 1988, Jim won All-America honors, the Big Ten Jesse Owens Male Athlete of the Year Award, the Big Ten Conference Player of the Year Award, and the Sullivan Award. The Sullivan Award is given each year to America's top amateur athlete and Jim was the first baseball player ever to win it!

• When people doubted that Jim would be good enough to play in the major leagues, he joined a big league team without ever playing in the minor leagues. Only 14 players since 1965 had done that!

"He's amazing," says Tino Martinez. "He's a great lesson for everybody. A lot of people say they can't do things for various reasons. He shows you can do anything you want to if you set your mind to it."

Jim's secret is that he learned to believe in himself while he was growing up. "My mom and dad were great," he says. "They never said that I couldn't do this or that, even though I was one-handed. They encouraged me at every step. They never pushed me into sports. As a matter of fact, they always pushed academics on me. A few people tried to tell me that I wouldn't go far in sports, but I didn't listen to them. I always thought I would play pro ball. I didn't think about anything holding me back."

Physically challenged people all over the world have been inspired by what Jim has done. He has received thousands of letters from people who say his courage and determination have helped them believe that they can overcome a physical handicap and be successful, too. Parents often bring their handicapped children to ballparks to meet him, and the kids tell Jim that he is their hero.

Jim says it makes him feel good to hear that, but he does not think of himself as a hero or someone who is particularly courageous. "It's hard to say that what I have fun doing is courageous," Jim says. "Baseball is just a game. I pitch to win, not to be courageous."

Tim Mead, the Angels publicity director, says, "It's incredible the number of letters he gets from handicapped kids, and he's met with probably 45 or so of them when he's on the road. But he really wants to downplay it. He's not doing it for the publicity. He's doing it to help these kids."

"I'm trying to make a career out of something and people all of a sudden see me as a beacon," Jim says. "It's not something I want to run away from, but at the same time, it's not something I want to promote."

It has taken Jim time to accept an important responsibility that comes with his job: many people consider him a role model, especially for handicapped children. "I've become more comfortable with that as I get older," he says. "I don't like to say that I'm important, but being a role model for people to look up to makes what I do important. Maybe if young kids see what I've been able to do, it can help them a little bit. That makes my playing baseball all the more worthwhile."

Still, people do not always understand that Jim wants

to be thought of as a professional athlete, not someone who is special or different because he has a physical handicap.

"The attitude I have is that I'm the same as anyone else," he says. "I don't look at what I have as a handicap. A handicap is a limitation. I haven't been limited in any way. There is a slight disability in that I don't have any fingers on my right hand, but to me, that isn't a disability. I have the *ability* to play baseball. I've been awfully fortunate in the things I've been given."

One thing Jim has been given is plenty of attention, but it has not always made him feel fortunate. Newspapers, magazines, and TV shows have done many stories about him since he was in high school. Reporters have asked him about his handicap thousands of times. Sometimes their questions have been rude and insensitive. One reporter even asked Jim, "Is anyone else in your family deformed?"

Jim says he understands why people ask questions about his handicap and why they think of him as an inspiration. He knows that what he has achieved in sports is very rare. But he has often wished that people would pay more attention to his accomplishments and less to the fact that he does not have a right hand.

"I used to tell myself that I'm normal because I want to be thought of as normal," Jim says. "Everyone wants to be treated as normal, but I've grown up enough to know that being called a one-handed pitcher is not an insult. I realized that playing with one hand is different. It's not a negative. It hasn't hurt me, it just changed a few things."

Doug Rader, the manager of the Angels, says, "Jim has had to answer some of the dumbest, most undignified questions I have ever heard, but he has handled everything with dignity and grace. He may be one of the most remarkable individuals I've ever known in baseball. Beside it all, he's just a red-blooded kid who's one of the guys in the clubhouse."

Jim's teammates call him "Abby" and sometimes they kid him about his handicap. Jim doesn't mind because ballplayers always poke fun at each other. It is their way of showing that they accept and like each other. The Angels players truly respect Jim's talent and accomplishments.

When catcher Rick Turner became Jim's roommate during the 1989 season, he thought he would have to help Jim tie his shoelaces or open doors for him. He quickly learned that Jim could do all those things and many more.

"You don't have to ask Jim what he can't do," Turner says. "You just sit back and watch what he can do."

As a person, Jim is friendly, humble, intelligent, and kind. "Jim never talks negatively about himself or anyone," says Jim's father, Mike. "That's just his nature."

Jim lives a modest, quiet life. "My daily routine isn't much," he says. "I get up, run a couple of errands, and come to the yard. I play baseball."

Jim is single and he shares a condominium with his teammate Chuck Finley in Newport Beach, California. He drives a white Nissan Maxima and he likes pro basketball. His favorite team is the Detroit Pistons. The Piston players are known as "The Bad Boys" of the NBA because of their rough style of play. "I like the team, but I don't like their attitude," Jim says.

Many major league players are paid millions of dollars each season by their teams. Jim's salary was only $68,500 during his first season with the Angels and $100,000 during his second season. Yet Jim has turned down offers to do commercials that would have paid him thousands of dollars. To Jim, just playing a sport he loves is the best reward. That's why he personally answers his fan mail and gladly signs autographs for free. Many players do not sign autographs unless fans pay for them because they feel that collectors are making money from their autographs.

"Some days it seems like I have the best job in the world," Jim says. "Living in California down by the beach, playing baseball in the major leagues."

Jim doesn't take his wonderful lifestyle for granted, however. He does charity work to help handicapped kids. He visits them in hospitals and schools and gives them some very important advice: "There is a handicap if you think in your mind there is one. If you put that completely out of your mind and forget about it, then it won't be a handicap. A person with all the physical attributes in the world can be handicapped if he puts limitations in his mind on what he can do."

What Jim Abbott has done is remarkable, but he wants people to understand one important thing about him. "I'm just a pitcher. I'm not trying to prove anything to anybody except, maybe: don't let anything stop you from trying."

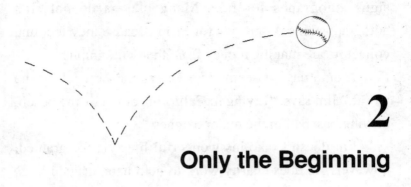

2

Only the Beginning

James Anthony Abbott was born on September 19, 1967, in Flint, Michigan. He was a normal, healthy baby in every way but one: he did not have a right hand. Jim's right arm ended halfway between his elbow and his wrist. On the end of that arm, there is only one tiny finger.

At first, Jim's handicap was a shock for his parents. His father Mike and his mother Kathy had just graduated from high school when Jim was born. They lived in an apartment in Flint and they did not have much money. Mr. Abbott worked in a meat-packing plant and later sold cars to earn a living. Mrs. Abbott could not work because she had to care for Jim, but she used her time at home to educate herself so that she could become a teacher. She went on to became a lawyer!

"If anybody had courage and strength, it was my mom and dad," Jim says. "They had me at 18 and 19 years old. It's tough trying to decide how to raise a kid at that age."

No matter how old a person may be, it is tough to decide how to raise a kid who is physically challenged. It is hard for parents to know how to help a handicapped child learn to live as normal a life as possible.

"I can only imagine what it would be like to have a wife who's pregnant and expecting a baby," Jim says. "There's so much hope and praying for a normal child, for him or her to live a normal life. If that doesn't happen, what a trauma that really must be: 'What do we do now? What's the right role model?' They feel like there's no standard for their children."

"We raised Jim by instinct," Kathy Abbott says.

Luckily for Mr. and Mrs. Abbott, Jim's handicap was not serious. He would be able to walk and talk and see. Jim could also be given a mechanical device called a prosthesis to wear on the end of his right arm and use as an artificial hand. "The doctor told us if Jim didn't have it, he wouldn't be able to do things like tie his shoes and use scissors," Kathy says.

Mr. and Mrs. Abbott knew that even if Jim wore a prosthesis, life would still be difficult for him. Handicapped children are often cruelly teased by "normal" kids who forget that no one chooses to be handicapped. Jim Abbott did not choose to be born without a right hand, just as you did not choose to be born with blue or brown or green eyes. Still, there were kids in Jim's neighborhood who taunted him by calling him "Stubs."

Jim was given a prosthesis when he was 4 years old. It was made of fiberglass and it had a metal hook on the end that opened and closed electronically. The prosthesis allowed Jim to pick up a pencil or hold a fork, but it felt clumsy. It also made him feel uncomfortable about himself. Sometimes strangers stared at him when they saw him on the street or in stores. The hook also frightened other kids when he started going to kindergarten.

"Even the teacher expressed concern that Jim might hurt somebody with the hook," Kathy says. "He was self-conscious about it. We told him it was the best thing for him, but we finally gave up and quit making him wear it."

Wearing a prosthesis did not keep Jim from being teased. There was a popular show on TV about a "bionic" man who was part human and part robot. "Other kids associated Jim and the bionic man with each other," Kathy says.

Jim stopped wearing the prosthesis for good when he was 8 years old. After that, the teasing seemed to stop. "Maybe I blocked it out in my own mind, but I don't remember anybody being cruel," Jim says. "Maybe there was something here and there, but it was more like calling someone wearing glasses 'Four Eyes.' "

Mr. and Mrs. Abbott treated Jim like any other child. They especially wanted him to have friends to play with. "My parents always encouraged me to be outgoing," Jim says. "My dad never wanted me to feel out of place. He never wanted me to be held back just because of my hand. My dad was always pushing me, when I'd see someone new, to walk up to the kid, shake his hand and say, 'Hi, my name is Jim Abbott.' He really encouraged that."

By being outgoing, Jim was able to make friends in school and in his neighborhood. "I think I had a very stable childhood," Jim says. "I still have friends that I've had since

the fourth grade. Right away, they accepted me and I accepted them."

Jim then became "one of the guys" in his neighborhood. Because his parents always encouraged him to try to
do new things, Jim was eager to play any game or sport that
his friends were playing. "Playing sports was a way to be
accepted by the kids I grew up with," Jim says. "My friends
loved to play, so I played."

One particular sport caught Jim's fancy when he was
6 years old. "Everyone on our block was playing baseball,
so I went home and told my dad that I wanted to play, too,"
he says.

Jim started playing catch with his dad to learn how to
catch and throw. "He told me to do whatever came naturally
to get the ball out of the glove and throw it back to him,"
Jim says. "I used the same catching and throwing system I
use now. It didn't take long to learn. I had no problems with
it and never thought about it while I was doing it. If there
were times when I got frustrated, it was because I wasn't
doing something I knew I could do, not something I couldn't
do."

Jim also learned to swing a baseball bat. He holds the

bat against the end of his right arm by wrapping his left hand around it and the bat handle.

Jim was soon practicing whenever he could. If his dad was busy, Jim would go to a large brick wall near his family's apartment. "I used to play catch by throwing a ball against the wall for hours at a time," he says. "I just had fun throwing the ball and catching the rebound. I would move closer and closer to the wall so I would have to be quicker and quicker because I had less time to react to the rebound. I'm sure all that practice had a lot to do with the fact that I can pitch a baseball and then quickly change my glove from hand to hand."

One of Jim's favorite things was pitching make-believe baseball games against the wall. "I was Nolan Ryan all the time in those games," he says. "The guys I idolized are Nolan Ryan, Orel Hershiser, people like that. I never said, 'Gee, I have one hand, so I'm going to admire Pete Gray.'"

Jim also practiced his baseball skills against his brother Chad, who is four years younger. "We had a game where we threw a tennis ball into a lawn chair and tried to hit it with a miniature bat," Jim says. "If you hit it into the trees, it was a home run. We played that game for hours."

Jim kept playing and practicing. Then one day he realized that he might be good enough to play Little League baseball. When Jim asked his parents if he could join a team, they hesitated. They thought he would be better off playing soccer because only goalies use their hands in that sport. Jim insisted that he wanted to play baseball.

"We laugh about it now. He didn't like soccer," Kathy says. "Chad is the soccer player. The one sport Jim doesn't need his hand for is about the only one he hasn't gravitated to."

Jim was 11 years old when he joined his first Little League team. At first, the players and coaches wondered how in the world a kid with one hand could ever play baseball, but Jim was given a chance to show what he could do. It was the turning point of his life.

"If someone had said, 'No, Jim, with that arm, maybe you should sit this out and keep score,' I might have been crushed and never gone on," he says. "Nobody ever said I shouldn't play. That was the key. If somebody had said no or discouraged me along the way, I would have stopped."

Jim dazzled his coaches and his teammates by throwing

a no-hitter in the first game he pitched! Word of this amazing young player spread quickly that season. The following year, there was a story about Jim in a local newspaper, *The Flint Journal*. His parents were surprised and amazed.

"We weren't aware of Jim's talent until a reporter called and said Jim was one of the best players in the league," Kathy says. "We hadn't been paying much attention to what he was doing. We just knew he was playing at the neighborhood fields and not getting into any mischief."

Jim was definitely not getting into any mischief. He was getting into the newspaper. That first no-hitter was only the beginning.

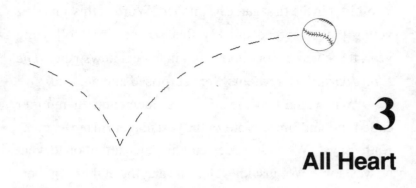

3

All Heart

Everyone, as Jim says, wants to be treated as a normal person. However, it is difficult for normal people to ignore the fact that handicapped people are different from them. As the years went by, Jim continued to shine in Little League and then Babe Ruth and Connie Mack baseball. Jim points out that most people began to forget about his handicap: "Not only my mom and dad, but my teammates, teachers, classmates, friends, coaches, everybody, almost to the point of ignoring it. I never heard anything about it. If anything at all came along that I couldn't handle, all anybody ever wanted to do was help."

Kathy Abbott says, "After a while, what he did we took

for granted, and all we did was let him do what he wanted. Jim has always been well-adjusted and self-motivated academically and in sports."

Jim loved sports. He played basketball and football in neighborhood games, but baseball was his true love. "Growing up, I always pictured myself as a baseball player," Jim says. "I never thought to myself, 'Wow, I only have one hand.' I just did things."

That amazed people who had doubts about him. Usually, those people were his coaches. "The coaches have been skeptical at every level," says Mrs. Abbott. "In junior high school, they told him he wouldn't be able to play in high school. He got to high school and everyone doubted that he would be able to play in college."

One of the doubters was Bob Holec, the baseball coach at Flint Central High School. One day when Jim was in junior high, Coach Holec watched him pitch in the city junior championship game. He was impressed by Jim's 80-mile-per-hour fastball, but, like many people, he wondered if Jim could field balls that were hit back at him.

"I was talking to Jim's father about that when a kid hit a high-hopper back to the mound," Holec says. "Jimmy threw him out. His father and I looked at each other and I said, 'I guess that answers that.'"

Jim entered Flint Central High as a ninth-grader in 1981 and played on the school's junior varsity baseball team. Opposing players and coaches were eager to test his fielding ability. Many teams bunted the ball softly toward the mound so that Jim would have to run in and field it. During the first game Jim pitched at Flint Central, eight opposing batters *in a row* bunted the ball! The first batter reached base safely, but Jim threw out the next seven.

Some people thought that Jim should have been insulted by what that team had done. "If I was in their shoes, I would try the same thing if I thought it would help me win," Jim said. "But I look at it as a pretty easy out myself. What irritates me is on real good bunts, when a batter would be safe anyway, people say, 'Well, it was his hand.'"

Jim played so well his first season in high school that he easily made the varsity baseball team as a sophomore. Coach Holec admired Jim's determination. "Jim is a tremendous competitor, but it's not because of his handicap," he told reporters. "Jimmy doesn't think he has a handicap."

That's why Jim joined an intramural basketball league

at Flint Central. He played forward and was one of his team's best scorers. Coach Holec then suspected that Jim might even be able to play football.

Flint Central's varsity football team needed a backup quarterback during Jim's junior year. Coach Holec asked Jim to give it a shot. "Football was a novelty to me," Jim says. "I went out for the team on a whim. My junior year was just a screw-around year. I mostly learned how to take the snap from the center."

Jim needed several weeks to master handling the snap from the center by placing his left hand underneath the ball and his right arm on top. He then brought the ball up to his chest and gripped the laces before he made his throw. Jim became so good at handling snaps that he did not drop one that year.

Jim also continued to sparkle on the baseball diamond. He pitched and played outfield. In one game, he threw a speedy runner out at home with a 270-foot throw from leftfield. Jim was a terror at the plate, too. He won a game that season by hitting a 330-foot home run. And when he played badly, he did not get discouraged.

One day, Jim pitched poorly in the first game of a

doubleheader. After the game, he spent some time talking quietly with a handicapped kid who was sitting in the stands. Jim then went out and won the second game for Flint Central by smacking a three-run homer!

Jim's senior year in high school was truly special. He was promoted to starting quarterback and led the varsity football team to a 10-2 record. In the semifinals of the state tournament, Jim fired four touchdown passes to lead Flint Central to a 26-20 win over Midland High School. He also averaged 37.5 yards as the team's punter that season and he was featured on "The NFL Today" television show.

"I honestly feel Jim is good enough as an athlete that if his first love was football, he could have been a quarterback at the college level," says Joe Eufinger, who was Flint Central's football coach.

That winter, Jim led his intramural basketball league in scoring. The following spring, he attracted more attention with his performances on the baseball team. He began the season by striking out 16 batters while pitching a no-hitter against Swartz Creek High School. He threw three more no-hitters that spring. In one of them, the opposing team hit only two of his pitches into fair territory!

Jim's record that season was 10-3 with a 0.75 earned run average. That means he gave up an average of less than one run in every nine innings he pitched! He also struck out 148 batters in 72.1 innings. When he wasn't pitching, Jim played first base, shortstop, and leftfield. At bat, he was just as awesome as he was on the mound. Jim batted .427 that season with 7 home runs and 31 RBIs. One of his homers traveled 400 feet!

Naturally, Jim attracted the attention of major league scouts, but some doubted that a one-handed pitcher would be able to play in the major leagues. One scout who thought otherwise was Don Wilke of the Toronto Blue Jays.

"He was a great guy," Jim says. "He said I had a major league fastball and also major league heart. I don't know if I agree with him about the major league heart, but I guess he was impressed with the way I threw the ball in the spring. He told me that I could work on a few things like the hard line drives hit back at me and turning the double play on some of those balls. He was very positive."

Bud Middaugh, the head baseball coach at the University of Michigan, was also very positive. "I hadn't really heard about the one-handed stuff," Coach Middaugh says.

"I recruited him because he can help our program."

When Coach Middaugh visited Flint Central, Jim was thrilled that Michigan was interested in him. The Michigan Wolverines were Jim's favorite college football, basketball, and baseball teams. Michigan's baseball teams had won four Big Ten Conference Championships for Coach Middaugh and Jim had dreamed of pitching for the Wolverines.

Oddly, Coach Holec told Jim that he might be better off playing for a smaller college where the competition would not be as tough. Jim didn't listen. He had his heart set on pitching for a major college, especially his favorite one.

That spring, Jim had a big decision to make. In late May, a week or so before the major league player draft, Toronto Blue Jays General Manager Pat Gillick called Jim's parents. He told them the Jays wanted to draft Jim, but he would not be chosen until a late round because there were questions about his ability to play in the big leagues. Gillick asked Mr. and Mrs. Abbott if Jim would be embarrassed if he was chosen late in the draft. The Abbotts replied that Jim wanted to be drafted, and he didn't care when.

On June 3, 1985, the Blue Jays chose Jim in the 36th round of the major league draft. They flew Jim to Toronto and offered him $50,000 to sign a minor league contract.

The fact that a one-handed pitcher had been drafted by a major league team was big news. Jim was questioned by reporters often during his weekend in Toronto. "The Blue Jays say they didn't take me because I was special," Jim explained. "They took me because they think I can pitch in the majors. I think I can too. It won't be easy, but it is possible. I'm not handicapped. I'm just a pitcher, the same as anyone else. I'm better than some, not as good as others."

Jim also talked about what being drafted meant to him. "I've grown up daydreaming about pitching in the majors, just like any kid might," he said. "I can imagine myself in a starting rotation with Orel Hershiser and Fernando Valenzuela. You know, 'Now starting for the Los Angeles Dodgers, Jim Abbott.' But if it never happens, it will be because I'm not good enough, not because I've got this hand."

Of course, Jim's other dream was to go to college. So he told the Blue Jays he needed time to decide if he wanted to play pro ball or accept a baseball scholarship.

"We've been very cautious," Mrs. Abbott told reporters. "We've tried to instill in Jim that he's got to think beyond baseball and get his education. I don't think he's ever been overconfident that he's going to make it to the majors."

A week or so later, Jim announced that he would be attending the University of Michigan. "It was a very tough decision," he said. "What I had in front of me were two dreams. I always wanted to pitch for the University of Michigan. But then this came along and I said, 'Jim, you have an opportunity to pitch professional baseball. You've dreamed about this.' But I still had a lot to prove to a lot of people, including myself. And if it turned out that I was wrong about my ability, then at least I would have gained a college education in the process."

Coach Middaugh was happy that Jim would be pitching for the Wolverines. "I think Jim's good enough to come in and pitch as a freshman," he said. "Jimmy throws in the mid-80's and if you can get a lefty throwing that fast, it's pretty good."

As a member of the Wolverines, Jim would prove to be much better than pretty good.

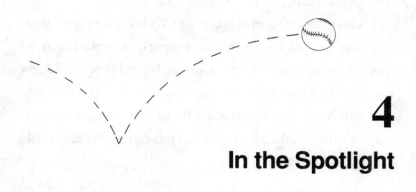

4

In the Spotlight

Jim was very excited when he arrived at Michigan's campus in Ann Arbor in September of 1985. "It's such a great opportunity to come here," he said. "I told myself after high school that everything else down the line was a bonus. I'm living out a dream down here at the University of Michigan. I wouldn't trade places with anybody in the whole world right now."

Jim was absolutely thrilled when he went to the University of Michigan Fieldhouse for the first time. "I got here for my first practice and they have all the best equipment, a great locker room," he said. "I looked down at my uniform shirt and it said 'University of Michigan.' I just couldn't believe it." For Jim, it really was a dream come true.

Over the years, more than 100 Wolverine players have gone on to play in the major leagues. Among the most successful are third baseman Chris Sabo and shortstop Barry Larkin. Both are stars for the Cincinnati Reds. Jim was aware of Michigan's reputation for producing major league players, but he said that, for him, a pro career, "is just a wild fantasy right now."

The Wolverines were a strong team that had won 55 games and lost only 10 the previous season. It didn't take long for Jim to recognize how talented his teammates were, especially outfielder Casey Close and first baseman Hal Morris. Both players were later drafted by the New York Yankees. Morris now plays for the Cincinnati Reds. "The level of competition is so much higher here," Jim said. "It's like the major leagues compared to high school."

Making the Wolverines starting pitching rotation was Jim's goal. He knew it would be a challenge, but he had faith in himself. "I never had any doubts about my arm," he said. "I never worry about having one hand. I have more of the doubts that everybody else has: worrying about the competition. Am I good enough to play on the Big Ten level? My arm never really enters into my thinking."

Jim was given his first test when the Wolverines flew to Florida to open the 1986 season against Villanova. Reporters and TV crews were there to cover the game, but unfortunately, Jim's first start wasn't very memorable. He was pitching wild and was taken out of the game in the second inning after he walked five batters. The Wolverines won anyway, 7-2.

Jim pitched poorly again in his second start. Coach Middaugh knew why. "There's so much attention on Jim every time he pitches," he said. "It'll take him a little time to settle down."

Coach Middaugh decided that Jim would get over his jitters more quickly if he spent some time as a relief pitcher. Relievers are less likely to worry about their next game because they never know when they will be asked to pitch again. As Coach Middaugh had hoped, Jim calmed down and got his first win after he was brought in to pitch in the top of the eighth inning of a game against the University of North Carolina (UNC).

UNC had runners on first and third, the score was tied 3-3, and there were two outs. Jim threw a ball and two strikes to the first hitter he faced. Then the runner on third tried to dash home as the Wolverine catcher tossed the ball back to Jim. The runner thought Jim wouldn't be able to catch the ball and get it out of his glove in time to throw home. Surprise! The runner was out at home by 20 feet!

"If they had done that on any of my other pitchers, they might have got away with it," Coach Middaugh said. "But Jim's much more aware. He was looking right at third base."

The Wolverines later rallied to win the game 6-3.

"I was relieved, to tell you the truth," Jim replied after he was asked how it felt to get his first win. "I was having some control problems at the time. I just got the ball, threw it right back, and the runner was out. It was great."

After the game against UNC, the Wolverines returned to Michigan with a 7-2 record. Their next game was at home in Ray Fisher Stadium against Grand Valley State College. Jim relieved starting pitcher Scott Kamienicki in the fourth inning and retired all 12 batters he faced. Michigan won 7-0. Jim had his second win.

Jim returned to the role of starting pitcher against the University of Miami in Ohio several days later. He retired the first nine batters he faced. Then the roof caved in. Jim was pounded for five runs and was taken out of the game in the fourth inning. Luckily, Michigan hung on to win 6-5.

Jim's rough start was made even tougher because of the tremendous amount of attention he was receiving from the media. He was asked to appear on *The Phil Donohue Show* and *Good Morning America*. Cable TV networks such as CNN and ESPN did feature stories about him. It's embarrassing to fail when the entire country is watching you.

After Jim pitched a three-hit shutout to beat Western Michigan 1-0, he was hit hard by the University of Minnesota in a game that was televised nationally. The 7-2 defeat was the first loss of his college career.

"Jim's had an extreme amount of tension since he's been here," Coach Middaugh explained. "He's handled everything really well."

In time, Jim settled down and improved. He beat Purdue, Indiana, and Michigan State to boost his record to 5-2. The Wolverines went on to capture the Big Ten Eastern Division Championship by beating Ohio State four games to none in a playoff.

The next step was the playoffs for the Big Ten Championship. After Michigan beat Wisconsin and Minnesota in the first two games, Coach Middaugh made Jim his relief pitcher in the third inning of the conference championship game. Jim came through with flying colors. He struck out 10 Minnesota batters and did not allow a hit until the eighth inning. The Wolverines won the conference title, 9-5, and Jim was the winning pitcher.

Jim's first season had been full of ups and downs, but he had done well. His final record was 6-2 and he had a 4.11 earned run average. Perhaps best of all, he had made only one fielding error all season. The error was a bad throw he made as he tried to pick a runner off base, but all pitchers make bad pickoff throws from time to time. Jim was named to the Big Ten All-Tournament Team and the Philadelphia Sportswriters Association named him the Most Courageous Athlete for 1986.

"The other night I watched a movie, *Something For Joey*, about football star John Cappelletti and his brother," Jim told the audience at the sportswriters dinner the night he received the award. "Now, that kind of stuff, what his brother went through dying of leukemia (a blood disease), was a lot more courageous than anything I've gone through."

Toward the end of Jim's first season at Michigan, the fuss that had been made about his handicap began to lessen. "The curiosity, the one-handed issue, I guess it will always be there, but it has kind of died down," Jim said. "A lot of people are tired of hearing about it. I like that. I'm tired of hearing about it."

People would hear about Jim's handicap more than ever during his sophomore season. But they would hear about it for a very good reason: Jim was phenomenally successful that year.

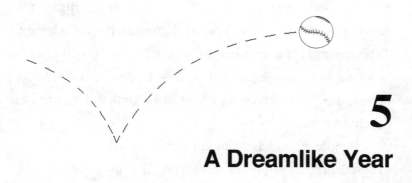

5

A Dreamlike Year

Jim got off to a hot start his sophomore year at Michigan. He won 9 of his first 10 starts and pitched 31 innings in a row without allowing a run. He threw shutouts against Purdue University and Ohio State, and a one-hitter against Illinois. The Wolverines' record that season was 50-10 and they won the Big 10 Championship again. Jim led the team in victories with 11 and was named the Wolverines' Most Valuable Player.

Jim's superb season drew raves from his coaches, his teammates, and major league scouts. "Very impressive," said Steve Boros, a scout for the San Diego Padres. "Good stuff. Live fastball. Decent curve. Throws strikes. If he stays healthy, he'll be a legitimate draft choice."

Bob Gardner, a scout for the California Angels, said, "Jim has the tools to pitch in the majors. What really amazes me is how he fields."

Jim had made only two errors all season. "He fields better than I do," said his teammate, Michigan pitcher Mike Ignasiak.

Jim received a great deal of praise, but he did not stop trying to improve. "I've been working on a 'slurve,' a pitch that is half-slider, half-curve," he said. "And I'm working on a change-up. Those are the things I'm working on: my weaknesses."

The more spectacular Jim was on the pitcher's mound, the more he heard that he had become a hero to handicapped people all over the country. "People write me letters calling me an inspiration and saying how courageous I am," he said. "I just try to pitch. I don't try to be inspirational or anything. I'm learning more and more that the one-handed pitcher has its place. If it helps a youngster or an adult overcome something, it makes me happy."

Jim made the Wolverines happy when they met Rider College in the National College Baseball Tournament on

May 22, 1987. The Wolverines had already lost a game in the tournament and would be eliminated if Rider beat them. On a hot, humid afternoon in Atlanta, Georgia, the Wolverines counted on Jim to keep their championship hopes alive. No sweat.

Jim allowed only eight hits and pitched his third shutout of the season as Michigan routed Rider, 10-0. In spite of the heat, Jim got stronger as the game went along. Only two Rider base runners got as far as third base during the game, none of them after the third inning. "I'm amazed that he was able to go the distance," said Coach Middaugh.

"I'm sure he'll be a major league prospect," said Sonny Pittaro, Rider's head coach. "He's one of the better ones you're going to see."

Michigan ended up losing to Georgia, 10-8, in its next game. Nevertheless Jim had become one of the top pitchers in college baseball. He was rewarded that June with an invitation to play for Team USA in the 1987 Pan Am Games. Like the Olympics, the Pan Am Games are an international event that is held every four years in different cities around the world. The Pan Am Games feature such sports as swimming, gymnastics, track and field, basketball, and baseball.

Jim's first task was to convince head coach Ron Fraser of Team USA that his handicap did not affect his ability to play. "Ron called and asked the same questions that everyone else does," Coach Middaugh said. "I told him not to take Jimmy because of the attention he would receive, but because he would be one of the team's better players."

Coach Fraser explained, "His coaches at Michigan were selling him just like any coach sells one of his own players. But I keep thinking these seasoned international players will bunt this kid to death. How can he switch the glove to get it up there in time to catch a line drive? No way!"

When Jim joined Team USA that summer, Coach Fraser immediately tested him by ordering the entire team to bunt against Jim in practice. Jim passed the test easily.

"He proved me wrong," Coach Fraser said. "When I brought him to the trials, it was more curiosity than anything. I didn't take it seriously. I knew the competition would be the best in the world, better than any college teams."

Team USA prepared for the Pan Am Games by playing 34 exhibition games that summer. Jim won 8 and lost only 1 and he had 51 strikeouts in 47.2 innings pitched. He quickly became the center of attention on the team, especially after Team USA beat Cuba for the first time since 1952.

When Jim took the mound for the game in Havana, Cuba on July 18, 1987, he received a standing ovation from a crowd of 50,000 fans. The Cuban people had heard all about Jim, but they had not yet seen him pitch.

"He's all they wanted to see," Coach Fraser says. "They wanted to see how he could switch the glove and throw. Well, the first batter hits a chopper 20 feet in the air down the third base line. Jim catches the ball on the back of his glove and throws the guy out. Another standing ovation. I don't think they took him seriously. They looked at him as a handicapped guy. Their attitude was, 'The U.S. wasn't able to beat us with their best. Now they come with a guy with one hand.'"

Jim made the Cubans take him seriously that day, though. He pitched a three-hitter to beat a team that many people thought was the best amateur baseball team in the world. What's more, Jim became the first pitcher from the U.S. in 25 years to beat Cuba!

"Whenever I pitch someplace for the first time, the reaction is the same," Jim said after the game. "But you have to remember, when my father came up with this idea, nobody had beating the Cubans in mind. It was just to play catch in the backyard. But now it's come to this."

Jim's victory that day made him a national hero in the eyes of the Cuban people. He was greeted after the game by Cuban President Fidel Castro, who playfully swatted Jim on the head. "I don't speak Spanish," Jim says, "but I think he said 'Good job,' or something like that."

"He's a very good pitcher," said Higino Velez, Cuba's head coach. "We admire him for his special dedication and intensity."

The Cuban people admired Jim so much that they followed him wherever he went while Team USA was in Cuba. "It was a great honor to be recognized," he says.

Coach Fraser added, "They'll be talking about him twenty years from now. He was no longer a freak. He was a pitcher, a real pitcher."

The Pan Am Games began on August 8, 1987, in Indianapolis, Indiana. The opening ceremonies were held at the Indianapolis Motor Speedway. When the U.S. team marched out to take its place among the teams from other countries, it was Jim who carried the American flag.

Jim was given that honor after he was chosen from a

group of worthy candidates that included diving champion Greg Louganis and basketball star David Robinson. "This is a feeling that I don't know I can describe to you," Jim told reporters after he learned he had been chosen to carry the flag. "To call home and tell your mom and dad you'll be carrying the flag for the United States. They went crazy. I don't know what to say. To be selected by the representatives of all the U.S. teams here is incredible."

Team USA's first game was against Nicaragua. The first half-inning lasted 32 minutes as the United States sent 14 batters to the plate. The first eight got hits, and first baseman Tino Martinez smashed a three-run homer. Team USA took a quick 10-0 lead.

The first Nicaraguan batter to face Jim bunted, but Jim threw him out easily. Jim then cruised through the next five innings, allowing only four hits and striking out six batters. The game was later stopped after seven innings because of a "mercy rule" that takes effect if a team is leading by 10 runs or more after seven innings. Team USA was leading 18-0! Jim was named the winning pitcher. It had been a very special day.

"I've never run across a feeling on a baseball field quite

like that," Jim said after the game. "When you're out there, and the National Anthem is playing, and you're holding your hat to your heart. It feels great."

As the Pan Am Games continued, Jim was repeatedly asked by reporters about his handicap. He received so much attention that his teammates began to make jokes. One day, while Team USA was doing stretching exercises before a game, assistant coach Bud Kelley ordered the players to touch their toes with both hands. "You, too, Abbott," Kelley said with a grin. Jim grinned back.

Jim politely and patiently answered all the questions he was asked, but the subject of his handicap grew tiresome. "I don't even think about it until you guys come around to remind me," he told reporters one day. "Everyone has limitations. It's just that mine are different than most people's. So I learned to do things differently. When you're little, learning to tie your shoes isn't easy for anyone. But you learned and so did I. I just learned to do it a little differently than you do."

When Jim was asked continually how he handles line drives that are hit back at him, he joked, "I just duck. Seriously, there are some plays that are just tougher for pitchers to make than others. I know a lot of pitchers who have as much trouble as I do with line drives and bunts."

Even with all the media coverage Jim received, there were still some fans who did not recognize him, and would not have guessed he was a baseball player. "You get kids asking for autographs," he said. "When they get to me, you can hear them asking, 'Should I get his?' I want to tell them, 'I pitch! I pitch!'"

Actually, Jim pitched very well. In three appearances at the Pan Am Games, he won two games and did not allow an earned run. He defeated Canada with a three-hitter in the semifinal game, but Team USA lost to Cuba in the finals and had to settle for the silver medal. The loss was disappointing, but Jim had been the biggest story of the Pan Am Games.

"How far he'll go, I don't know," Coach Fraser said. "He may be a major leaguer or a minor leaguer, but you know he'll give it 100 percent to get there. I'm pulling for him. He's touched my life."

Two months later, Jim flew to New York City for an award ceremony. He was one of nine nominees for the "Golden Spikes Award." Each year, the award is given to the top amateur baseball player in the United States.

Jim was up against stiff competition. Some of the other nominees were outfielder Ken Griffey, Jr., third baseman Robin Ventura, and pitchers Jack McDowell, Derek Lilliquist, and Cris Carpenter. Like Jim, each of those players went on to play in the major leagues.

The winner of the Golden Spikes was announced at a press luncheon at the Downtown Athletic Club. The winner was . . . Jim Abbott!

"It makes me very proud," Jim said after he received the award. "I know a lot of people had a great year and I never considered myself a candidate." A majority of the 60-member panel from the United States Baseball Federation thought differently.

The Golden Spikes was the first of two important awards Jim won for his fine performance in 1987. The second was the James E. Sullivan Award. The Sullivan is given to America's top amateur athlete each year by the Amateur Athletic Union. Such famous athletes as diver Greg Louganis and track stars Carl Lewis, Mary Decker, and Jackie Joyner-Kersee have also won it. Jim was the first baseball player ever to win the Sullivan!

Jim was selected for the award over some very worthy candidates. World hurdling champion Greg Foster, swimming champion Janet Evans, and college basketball star David Robinson were among the nominees. Jim was flabbergasted when his name was announced on March 7, 1988, at the award ceremony in Indianapolis.

"I'm in shock!" Jim told the audience at the Indiana Convention Center that evening. "If you asked me a year ago, I wouldn't have thought any of this would happen to me. It's just incredible. I just thought I was coming here to a dinner and to meet some of these other athletes. When I heard my name, it almost knocked me off the chair. This is the culmination of a dream-like year."

Jim was asked if he thought he had been given the award because of what he had done in spite of his handicap. "I would like to think that it was based purely on my ability, but I'm sure my situation had a lot to do with it," he replied. "Still, that's good, because if anybody got something extra out of my playing baseball and it helped them with their life, then I'm pleased."

Gymnast Scott Johnson, who was also a finalist for the award, said, "Jim's not only a great athlete, but a great person with courage. He's a great pitcher. I don't think he won the award because he has a handicap. I respect him for his accomplishments."

As far as accomplishments were concerned, Jim Abbott was just warming up.

6

A Hard Act to Follow

The Sullivan Award made Jim the most famous college baseball player in the United States. He received more attention than ever before and greater things were expected of him. Much was written and said about his chances of being drafted by a major league team or being chosen to pitch for the U.S. Olympic baseball team. Jim did not let all the attention go to his head.

"I don't feel like a celebrity," Jim said. "I just want to pitch as well as I can for Michigan and get to the college world series."

The 1988 college baseball season began only four days after Jim won the Sullivan Award. He wanted very much to show that he deserved it, but he tried too hard. In his first start of the year, Jim was hit hard by the Texas Longhorns. He continued to struggle during the first half of the season and ended up allowing more walks (47) and hits (79) than he ever had before in his college career.

"It became a downward spiral," Jim says. "I expected a lot of things to come naturally and they didn't."

Coach Middaugh never lost faith in Jim. He kept Jim in the Wolverines' starting rotation and Jim rewarded his coach's patience with a 9-3 record and a 3.03 earned run average.

"A lot is expected of one who has received so much attention," Coach Middaugh said during the season. "He's disappointed with the way he's pitched, but he's handled it well."

Luckily, Jim's inconsistent performance did not hurt his chances of being chosen in the major league draft. "He has a good arm and poise," said Harry Dalton, the general manager of the Milwaukee Brewers. "He's a good prospect."

Jim was relieved to hear that, but he wanted to keep his mind on helping the Wolverines. "Everybody wants to play major league baseball," Jim said. "I'd love to get my shot. If I do get an opportunity, I'll try to make the best of it. But right now, the draft is on the back burner."

Jim was also affected by a bad cold he had trouble shaking, and he was distracted by all the attention he was receiving. Thousands of letters poured in from parents who had handicapped children. They wrote to tell Jim how much his success and example meant to them and their children. Jim often felt uneasy about that.

"I really can't say much to the parents who write," Jim said. "It's hard for me to think of myself as a role model. I've just told them to tell the children what I've always believed — that you can do anything you want if you put your mind to it."

Yet another distraction was the talk that Jim would be leaving Michigan before graduation to play pro baseball. He was majoring in Communications and despite the rumors, he realized the importance of getting an education. Making a choice between a college degree and a pro career was not something Jim wanted to deal with at that point.

"First I have to get back in my groove," he said. "But yes, I'm thinking of playing professionally. I've never imagined not going on to pro baseball."

Jim worked harder on his weaknesses as the season progressed. Whenever he pitched poorly, he tried to think about the times he had done well. "I've been working on my breaking pitch and on moving it in and out on hitters," he said. "I think one of my assets is that I have a lot of confidence in my ability. That Cuba game did a lot for my self-confidence. I thought, 'Wow! I can beat anybody I want.'"

It was hard to disagree after Jim pitched back-to-back shutouts against Purdue University and Adrian College. He also put together two streaks in which he did not allow a run. The first streak lasted 15 innings, the second lasted 25.1 innings.

The Wolverines finished the 1988 season with a 48-19 record. They failed to reach the college world series, but Jim was named Michigan's Most Valuable Pitcher by his team-mates. Other awards and honors came rolling in. He was chosen as an All-America, the Big Ten Male Athlete of the Year, and the Big Ten Player of the Year.

As the major league draft approached that June, it seemed likely that Jim would be one of the first 15 players chosen. Yet some teams were nervous about drafting him. A physically handicapped player had never been chosen in the 24-year history of the draft.

"I thought I'd be drafted pretty high," Jim said, "but I can understand that thinking. My stock went down because I had a rocky season at Michigan. My concentration wasn't that good after the Sullivan Award."

The old bugaboo about Jim's fielding also rose again. "What concerns a lot of scouts is that he'll get hit by balls up the middle as he tries to put his glove onto his left hand," said a major league executive.

The California Angels, however, were sold on Jim's ability. They knew their chances of drafting him would be better if other teams had doubts.

On June 1, 1988, the Angels chose Jim in the first round of the draft. Four pitchers were taken ahead of him, but he was the eighth player chosen overall. The Angels clearly thought that Jim was special.

"Jim's the only pitcher we ever drafted that we knew going into the draft what he had inside," said Bill Bavasi, the Angels' minor league director.

"We looked very closely at the fielding aspect," said

Angel scout George Bradley. "We analyzed it and cross-checked it. We had a lot of people watch him and the consensus is that he handles it very well. He can field bunts and defend his position, and when we concluded that fielding was not a factor, we decided that he was *the* left-hander in the draft. He's got the best fastball we've seen. He's the best all-around pitcher we've seen. And we felt that he was far enough along that it won't take him as long to get to the majors as some of the other pitchers available."

Jim was especially happy that the Angels had drafted him. "If I had made a list of the organizations I'd like to play for, the Angels would have been very high on it," he said. "And being the eighth player picked is an honor. It's personally gratifying because these are the pros and I was picked in the first round solely on my ability. It sounds a little phony, but all these things let me know how lucky I've been."

Jim's selection by the Angels started a debate about a handicapped person's ability to play successfully in the major leagues. Some people even accused the Angels of drafting Jim as a publicity stunt. They recalled how in 1951 the St. Louis Browns entertained their fans by sending a midget named Eddie Gaedel up to bat in a game. However, there was one expert on handicapped players who gave Jim a vote of confidence.

"I've watched him pitch on television and he looks like a very good pitcher," said Pete Gray, the one-armed outfielder who played for the St. Louis Browns in 1945. "And the fact that he has only one hand doesn't seem to affect him."

Jim, of course, agreed. "Hitters don't bunt on me any more than any other pitcher," he said. "I don't know what they'll do on the next level up, but I'm looking forward to the opportunity to prove that there isn't much difference."

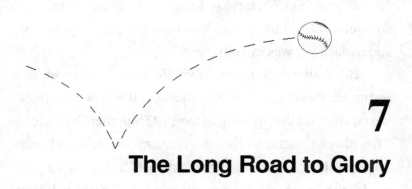

7
The Long Road to Glory

Before Jim began his major league career, he was given another wonderful opportunity in the spring of 1988. He was one of 40 college players who were invited to try out for the U.S. Olympic baseball team. Jim reported to the team's training camp in June after school ended.

"The Olympics are something I'd really like to do," he said. "We had a lot of fun [at the Pan Am Games] last summer and it's a whole different feeling when you're representing your country."

Jim's experiences with Team USA during the summer of 1988 were memorable to say the least. "We were on the road from June 10th until the end of September," he says.

"It was grueling. We were in foreign countries, eating food we weren't used to eating. You couldn't find anything in some places. It was awfully hard."

Baseball was only an Olympic exhibition sport and teams were awarded unofficial medals. (It will be an official medal sport for the first time at the 1992 Summer Olympics.) That did not matter to Jim and his teammates. It had been 14 years since a baseball team from the U.S. had won a gold medal at a major international tournament. That fact did not sit well with many Americans who did not like seeing other countries beating the U.S. in a sport that is known as "America's National Pastime."

Team USA set up camp at a naval base in Millington, Tennessee, and head coach Mark Marquess ran the team's daily four-hour practices like a drill instructor. "Move those puppies!" he yelled whenever he wanted his players to hustle.

The hard work made Team USA better and more disciplined. The players also became close friends because they were rarely allowed to leave the base.

"We were stuck there," says third baseman Robin Ventura. "We stayed in barracks. We had no cars, nothing to do. We played basketball one day and that lasted about 10 minutes. It was about 110 degrees. You're bored, so you have to interact with one another. Then when you go to Japan to play, it's easy to stick together. It's the way you survive."

In late June, Team USA flew to Japan to play five exhibition games. On June 29, a crowd of 20,000 fans in the city of Sendai saw Jim pitch five shutout innings against a team of Japanese all-stars. He allowed only one hit and struck out seven. Team USA lost, 4-3, but the Japanese team could see that Jim had improved a great deal. "I was stunned to see his fastball become so much faster in one year," said Yukichi Maedo, who had coached against Jim in 1987 at the Pan Am Games.

Jim had been working very hard. He knew he would be facing some of the best amateur teams in the world and that he would have to pitch smartly and aggressively to win. "I think you develop to the level of your competition," Jim said. "You learn to do what your competition forces you to learn. When I went to Michigan, I only had a fastball. Then I had to add the curve and the cut fastball, which is my slider. Now, I'm working on an off-speed curve and a straight change-up. I'm working on pitching inside," he said. "That's the big thing for me in the future and I know that I have to learn to do it."

Team USA won two of its five games in Japan. Jim pitched in three of them and gave up a total of only four hits and no earned runs. Coach Marquess was very impressed. "As a person, they told me Abbott was the All-American boy — almost too good to be true," he said. "But he's surprised me. He's better than that. I expected him to be a polished left-hander. What I didn't know is that right now, Jim's the hardest thrower on my staff."

That was a special honor. Team USA's pitching staff included such flamethrowers as Andy Benes, Ben Mc-Donald, and Pat Combs. All three could throw a fastball 90 miles per hour and they are now star pitchers in the major leagues.

Team USA returned to the United States to play 29 games in several cities against teams from Taiwan, Korea, and Cuba. They won 22 of them, even though they often had to get up at 4:15 in the morning and take six-hour bus rides to games.

The biggest test came in a seven-game series against

Tony Tomsic / Sports Illustrated

During his senior year in high school, Jim was offered a baseball scholarship to the University of Michigan. He was also drafted by the Toronto Blue Jays. It was a tough decision for Jim to make, but in the end he decided that it was important to get a good education. He joined the Wolverines for the 1986 season.

John McDonough / Sports Illustrated

In June of his sophomore year, Jim was invited to play for Team USA in the 1987 Pan Am Games. At Jim's first practice, head coach Ron Fraser tested his fielding ability by ordering the team to bunt against him. Jim passed the test easily and at Team USA's first game, he pitched his way to an 18-0 win over Nicaragua.

On September 28, 1988, Jim took the pitcher's mound in Chamsil Baseball Stadium for the final game against the Japanese team in the 1988 Olympic baseball tournament. Team USA had a 4-1 lead when Jim gave up two hits and two walks in the sixth. One of the walks forced a run because the bases were loaded. Then Japan scored another run off a failed double play, bringing the score to 4-3. Jim didn't allow another run that inning. Then, in the eighth, Team USA's Tino Martinez hit his second home run of the game and the score was 5-3. After that, it was easy.

The players on Team USA stood proudly as they received their gold medals and flowers while The Star Spangled Banner was played. All of the twenty-three young men who wore the gold that day were later drafted by major league teams.

Sullivan Award Winners 1980-1987

Year	Player	Sport
1980	Eric Heiden	Speed Skating
1981	Carl Lewis	Track
1982	Mary Decker	Track
1983	Edwin Moses	Track
1984	Greg Louganis	Diving
1985	Joan B. Samuelson	Track
1986	Jackie Joyner-Kersee	Track
1987	Jim Abbott	Baseball

Jim lost his second start with the Angels, 5-0, in a game against the Oakland A's in 1989. Bad weather and a case of the flu kept him out of the lineup until late April. Through it all, Angel pitching coach Marcel Lachemann stood by him.

Professional Debuts in the Major Leagues

Players who made their major league debuts without first playing in the minors.

Year	Player	Year	Player
1967	Mike Adamson	1973	Dave Winfield
1969	Steve Dunning	1978	Mike Morgan
1971	Pete Broburg	1978	Tim Conroy
1971	Burt Hooton	1978	Bob Horner
1972	Dave Roberts	1978	Brian Milner
1973	Dick Ruthven	1985	Pete Incaviglia
1973	David Clyde	1989	Jim Abbott
1973	Eddie Bane	1990	John Olerud

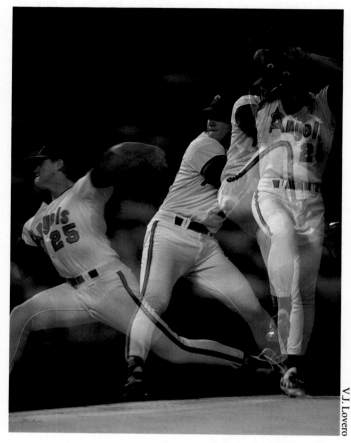

V.J. Lovero

*When Jim pitches, he balances his baseball
glove on the end of his right arm, throws the
ball, then quickly slides his left hand into the
glove so that he can catch the ball if it is hit or
thrown to him.*

V.J. Lovero / Sports Illustrated

One of the questions people have asked about Jim ever since he started playing Little League baseball at the age of 11 was whether he could field the ball. Jim has proved over and over that he can.

In 1989, only two left-handed players hit home runs off Jim Abbott. Who were they?

Don Mattingly and George Brett.

V.J. Lovero

During a 1990 Spring Training game against the Los Angeles Dodgers of the National League, Jim stepped up to the plate for a very rare chance at bat. American League pitchers never bat during the regular season.

V.J. Lovero / Sports Illustrated

Not all of the attention Jim received from the press was positive. Some reporters accused the Angels of letting Jim pitch as a way of attracting attention to the team. Jim responded by playing baseball well enough to prove that he was up to major league standards.

Two former New York Yankee slugging stars have been traded to the California Angels. Who were they?

Reggie Jackson and Dave Winfield.

V.J. Lovero

Doing laps with teammate and fellow pitcher Mark Langston is one way for Jim to escape the hordes of fans and reporters that seem to follow his every move.

V.J. Lovero

Looking like a modern-day Pied Piper, Jim is followed by young fans wherever he goes. An inspiration to people all over the world, Jim is especially popular with children.

Top Seasons for Angels' Lefty Pitchers

California had the unusual feature of having two or more lefthanded pitchers who won 10 or more games in:

Year	Players
1968	George Brunet and Clyde Wright
1971	Rudy May and Clyde Wright
1972	Rudy May and Clyde Wright
1978	Dave LaRoche and Frank Tanana
1989	Jim Abbott and Chuck Finley
1990	Jim Abbott and Chuck Finley

V. J. Lovero

After receiving so much attention during his rookie season, Jim Abbott of the California Angels spent more time working on his pitching skills. His record for his second season was 10-14 with a 4.51 ERA.

JIM ABBOTT HAS BEEN A TOUGH COMPETITOR ALL OF HIS LIFE. HE HAS ALWAYS CONCENTRATED ON PLAYING BALL, EVEN THOUGH HE WAS BORN WITHOUT A RIGHT HAND. HIS HARD WORK AND DETERMINATION HAVE MADE HIM A RISING STAR.

JIM JOINED THE LITTLE LEAGUE WHEN HE WAS 11, AND PITCHED A NO-HITTER IN HIS FIRST GAME!

IT WASN'T A FLUKE. DURING A HIGH SCHOOL GAME THAT JIM PITCHED, EIGHT BATTERS IN A ROW BUNTED. THE FIRST BATTER BEAT JIM'S THROW TO FIRST, BUT HE THREW OUT THE NEXT SEVEN BATTERS!

JIM ABBOTT PITCHED A TOUGH GAME AGAINST JAPAN AT THE SUMMER OLYMPICS IN 1988. TEAM USA WON THE GAME AND THE GOLD MEDAL, THE FIRST GOLD MEDAL AN AMERICAN BASEBALL TEAM HAD WON IN A MAJOR INTERNATIONAL TOURNAMENT IN 14 YEARS.

ON APRIL 24, 1989, JIM ABBOTT WON HIS FIRST MAJOR LEAGUE BALL GAME, BEATING THE BALTIMORE ORIOLES, 3-2.

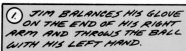

1. JIM BALANCES HIS GLOVE ON THE END OF HIS RIGHT ARM AND THROWS THE BALL WITH HIS LEFT HAND.

2. HE THEN SLIDES THE GLOVE ONTO HIS LEFT HAND TO CATCH THE BALL WHEN IT'S HIT BACK TO HIM.

3. ONCE HE HAS THE BALL, HE CRADLES HIS GLOVE IN THE CROOK OF HIS RIGHT ARM AND PULLS HIS HAND OUT.

4. NOW HE CAN GRAB THE BALL WITH HIS LEFT HAND AND THROW THE RUNNER OUT!

IF I DIDN'T SEE HIS MOVES MYSELF, I WOULDN'T HAVE BELIEVED ANYONE COULD DO THAT!

JIM ABBOTT'S HARD WORK AND POSITIVE ATTITUDE HAVE MADE HIM AN INSPIRATION TO PEOPLE EVERYWHERE. HE PROVES THAT NOTHING SHOULD STOP YOU FROM REACHING YOUR GOALS.

Cuba in mid-August. "Cuba is better than some major league teams, no question," Coach Marquess said.

Jim pitched the first game and Team USA beat Cuba 13-8. Then the Americans lost the next four games. Jim pitched well in the fifth game but lost a heartbreaker, 2-1, after a Cuban batter smoked one of his fastballs for a home run in the ninth inning. Team USA rallied to win the next two games 12-2 and 5-2. Coach Marquess was pleased by what he had seen.

"Actually, we could have won at least six of the seven games," he said. "I thought going in we would have a great pitching staff. Our real strength is the balance we have. We know we can win 2-1 because we have the speed to create runs. We can play great defense, and if we need to win 13-12, we can do that, too."

Next stop: the World Championships in Italy. Teams from 12 nations competed in the tournament, which lasted from August 22 to September 7. Each team in the tournament played a minimum of 11 games to get to the gold medal round. The two finalists were Cuba and Team USA.

It was a hard-fought showdown, but it ended in disappointment for the young U.S. team. In the first game, Cuba came from behind in the ninth inning to win, 10-9. In the second game, Jim took a three-hitter into the ninth inning, but Cuba rallied again to win, 4-3. Team USA settled for the silver medal.

The next day, Team USA checked out of its hotel in Parma, Italy, at 3:30 in the morning. The 23 players took a six-and-a-half-hour bus ride to Rome and caught a flight to New Delhi, India. After a wait of several hours, they boarded a flight for Tokyo, Japan. In Tokyo, they caught a flight to the Japanese city of Osaka. Then came a two-hour bus ride to Kobe.

Like his teammates, Jim was exhausted by the 30-hour trip. But what he saw when they arrived in Japan woke him up very quickly.

"When I first got off the plane in Tokyo, there must have been 50 or 75 cameramen waiting there," Jim recalls. "Every kind of camera, every kind of lens. I didn't know what was going on. All of a sudden, click-click-click. They were fascinated by my playing with one hand."

Jim was such a celebrity during his visit to Japan that his teammates started calling him "Abbott San." "San" is a Japanese word that means "sir."

"My picture was in the paper every day," he says. "There was a constant amount of attention. When we first practiced there, I fielded a bunt and cameras went off by the millions. Before I left, a lady gave me a scrapbook and there was a huge layout, frame by frame, of me turning my glove over while I made a fielding play."

When the Summer Olympics began in Seoul, South Korea, 9,626 athletes from all over the world were there to compete. Many of them, such as tennis player Steffi Graf, sprinter Carl Lewis, and swimmer Matt Biondi were already international stars. Jim was wide-eyed with excitement at finding himself in such famous company and he carried a camera wherever he went.

"You go down to eat in the cafeteria and every day you see a Biondi or a Steffi Graf," Jim said. "I had my picture taken with [tennis star] Gabriela Sabatini and that was real nice."

Jim was surprised to find that many of the other athletes knew who he was. One day, tennis star Pam Shriver spotted him in the Olympic Village and called out, "Happy Birthday!" Jim's teammates wondered how she knew that he had turned 21 years old that day.

The reason was that Jim was receiving more attention than any other Olympic athlete. He was cheered by hundreds of Korean kids the first time he took the field for practice at Chamshil Baseball Stadium. Reporters mobbed him wherever he went and asked him the same thing again and again:

Question: You have a chance to become the first one-handed person to ever pitch in the Olympics, Jim. How did you become good enough to get here?

Answer: "My parents have everything to do with my being here in the Olympics. From early on, they encouraged me to do everything. If they had told me, 'No, we don't think you can play ball,' I wouldn't be playing. That's one of the big things about me being here, giving pride back to my parents."

Question: How did you ever overcome your handicap?

Answer: "I don't look at it as overcoming something. My hand hasn't kept me from doing anything I wanted to do. I just learned to do it. It's not like learning to play basketball with two hands and then trying to play it with one. Hey, maybe my way is easier. Nobody really knows, do they?"

Question: Don't you have trouble fielding hard line drives that are hit back at you?

Answer: "I can talk about it until I'm blue in the face, but that doesn't prove anything. I still think I'm able to protect myself."

Question: How do you feel, Jim?

Answer: "If you had asked me a couple of days ago, I would have said I'm just really tired. Right now, I want to play baseball."

There were eight teams in the Olympic tournament: South Korea, Australia, Canada, Japan, Taiwan, Puerto Rico, the Netherlands, and the United States. (Cuba did not attend the Olympics for political reasons.) The teams were divided into two four-team divisions and each team played three games. Two teams from each division advanced to a one-game semifinal. The two winners of the semifinals played one game for the gold medal.

Team USA knew that it could not afford to lose more than once if it wanted to reach the gold medal game. "That's one of the points we've hammered at the kids since this team was put together," Coach Marquess said. "The way the Olympic tournament is structured, you can have the best team in creation and still not win if you can't hit some other country's best pitcher on a given day. The format doesn't prove who has the best team, just who has the best couple of pitchers."

Luckily, Team USA had three excellent pitchers. Right-hander Andy Benes of Evansville University had a 7-2 record and a 3.29 earned run average (ERA) during Team USA's 53 games that summer. Right-hander Ben McDonald of Louisiana State University had an 8-2 record and a 2.61 ERA. Jim's record was 8-1 with a 2.55 ERA.

Coach Marquess put a lot of thought into how he set up his starting rotation. Ben McDonald pitched the first game and lasted the full nine innings as Team USA beat South Korea 5-3. Andy Benes started the second game and the U.S. routed Australia 12-2. Jim started against Canada in the third game. He pitched three innings and struck out seven before Coach Marquess brought in a reliever. Canada then rallied to win the game 8-7.

The loss to Canada did not matter because Team USA had already qualified for the semifinals with two wins. Jim had been taken out so he could have extra time to rest in case he was needed to pitch the gold medal game.

On September 26, Ben McDonald beat Puerto Rico, 7-2, in the semifinals. It was now up to Jim to beat Japan for the gold medal.

Japan was a formidable opponent. At the 1984 Olympics, Japan had beaten a team from the U.S. that featured such current major league stars as Will Clark, Mark Mc-Gwire, Cory Snyder, Barry Larkin, and Bobby Witt.

"I asked the Japanese coach how his team compared to the one that won in 1984 and he said they are better now," Coach Marquess said. "I told our kids not to worry about stuff like that. I told them to enjoy the game, to play it only for themselves, not for the 1984 team or for me or for anyone else."

On September 28, 1988, Jim Abbott took the mound in Chamshil Baseball Stadium on a hot, sunny afternoon. A crowd of 29,600 fans were in the stands. Millions of other people watched on TV. Jim's opponent was Takehiro Ishii, Japan's best pitcher. Ishii had already won two games in Seoul, allowing only two hits in the 20 innings he pitched.

Japan scored the first run of the game in the second inning. Ishii held Team USA's hitters in check until the fourth inning, when Robin Ventura singled and Tino Martinez crushed a pitch for a 425-foot home run to centerfield. The next two batters hit singles and Ishii was taken out of the game. By the end of the inning, Team USA had a 3-1 lead.

Team USA increased its lead in the fifth inning when Martinez drove in another run with a single. Jim began to sense that victory was near, but when he took the mound in the sixth inning, he tried too hard to blow each hitter away. He lost his control and gave up two hits and two walks. One of the walks forced in a run because the bases were loaded.

"I was overthrowing the ball that inning, and I got a little bit out of synch," Jim says. "And about this time, my catcher was really starting to get on my case."

Jim could see that catcher Doug Robbins was upset. After each pitch, Robbins looked towards Team USA's dugout and shook his head. Coach Marquess told Andy Benes to start warming up. "I came pretty close to giving Jim the hook at that point," he said.

Japan scored another run when shortstop Dave Silvestri failed to turn a double play. The score was now 4-3. Jim bore down and started throwing strikes again. He got out of the inning without allowing any more runs.

In the top of the eighth inning, Tino Martinez gave Jim some breathing space by hitting a home run to leftfield. The score was now 5-3. "I really appreciated Tino's second homer because the Japanese aren't what you would call a 'long ball' type of team," Jim says. "So with a two-run lead, I didn't have to worry about getting beat."

Japan tried to fight back in their at-bat that inning. After the first batter singled, Jim snuffed Japan's rally by stopping a hard chopper up the middle before it went past him for a base hit. Jim threw the runner out at first and then retired the next two hitters. In the bottom of the ninth, Jim got three ground ball outs in a row to clinch the gold medal.

After he crawled out from under a pile of whooping teammates, Jim was warmly greeted by the Japanese team. He shook hands with each player while the other American players took a victory lap around the field. Then they received their medals and *The Star Spangled Banner* was played. Team USA had reached the happy end of a long, hard road.

"You start a summer with your mind on just one game: the game for the Olympic gold medal," Doug Robbins told reporters after the game. "You work hard to qualify for that one game and, finally, you do. And then, when that one game is played, you win it. What more can you ask?"

Jim agreed. "This is my Number One thrill in sports. There is something to be said about winning a gold medal in a team sport and going out and hugging and sharing it with everybody."

"I don't know how anything can top this," said Tino Martinez. "The nicest part will be running into Jimmy and the other guys in the major league parks the next few years. We'll look at each other and smile and share in the moment again."

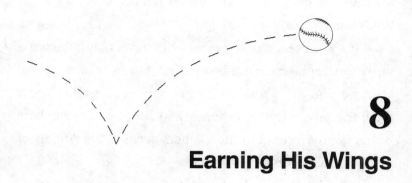

8

Earning His Wings

Jim arrived at the California Angels' spring training camp in Mesa, Arizona, on February 15, 1989. It didn't take him long to realize where he was. "Just looking around, it hits you," he said, remembering his first few days with enthusiasm. "A big league camp!"

The Angels needed left-handed pitchers and were willing to give Jim a chance to make the team, but he was expected to spend the season with the Angels' minor league team in Midland, Texas. After all, Jim was only 21 years old at the time and many pitchers that age need seasoning in the minors before they are ready to pitch in the big leagues.

"Jim is going to be in the big leagues for a long time,"

said Angels pitching coach Marcel Lachemann. "You just don't want to rush him."

Jim's presence in Mesa was big news that attracted a crowd of reporters. During his first two weeks at spring training, Jim did a total of 25 interviews. Not all of them were friendly. Some reporters asked Jim if other members of his family were deformed, others accused the Angels of using Jim as a publicity gimmick.

"I knew there would be a lot of press this spring," Jim said, "but, well, this is my own opinion. There is a different line of questions for professionals than amateurs. My hand seems to be such an issue. Some of the questions are almost hostile. It's a story, I understand. I can't explain it, but it seems like I'm public property now. All the questions have been about my hand. It doesn't seem to go beyond that."

Jim turned down offers to do commercials and write books about himself and made up his mind to work as hard as he possibly could toward his goal of making the Angels. As for all the hoopla about a one-handed pitcher trying out for a major league team, Jim said, "I'm hoping the novelty will wear off."

On March 3, 1989, Jim made his professional debut in

an exhibition game against the San Diego Padres in Yuma, Arizona. The contest was only a "B" game, which is like a junior varsity game, but it attracted so much attention that it had to be moved to Desert Sun Stadium, the Padres' main spring training field.

It was a windy day and the infield dust was blowing all over the place. Jim came in to pitch in the fourth inning and began blowing the Padres away. Tom Howard, the first batter, did not swing at an inside fastball that the umpire called for strike three. The next batter, shortstop Gary Green, struck out on three pitches. Jim then got two quick strikes on second baseman Joey Cora, but Cora hit a ground ball that was booted by the Angels shortstop for an error. Jim then retired the next four batters he faced and did not allow a hit until the sixth inning.

Jim pitched three innings that day and the Angels won 4-2. He allowed two hits, no runs, and he struck out four. Doug Rader, the Angels manager, was wild with joy. He rewarded Jim with a lemon drop and then gushed to reporters, "How about that first batter? Wham, wham, see you later! The level of Jim's maturity and his composure and his stability, I can't tell you how wonderful it is. All the accolades he's received are richly deserved."

The Padres were impressed too. "Jim's a great competitor, just to get here," said Padre infielder Tim Flannery. "But after three pitches, you forget all about that. You're just looking for the ball — and on that, he doesn't do anything different than anybody else. He's got a fastball that just takes off."

Flannery's teammate, outfielder Carmelo Martinez, said, "Everybody in the dugout is saying, 'Yeah, check this guy out.' For my first at-bat, it was hard to concentrate. But then you realize that the ball comes from the same place and goes to the same place. If you're just looking at his arm, he's got you."

After Jim finished his three innings of pitching, he was surrounded by microphones, TV cameras, tape recorders, reporters, and autograph seekers. "I'm happy," he told the crowd. "It's nice to get the first one out of the way, to show the club what I can do. I got rid of a bit of the jitters. Now I can build on this."

A reporter asked Jim if he thought he could make the team. "I don't know," Jim replied. "I never played professional baseball before. I don't know what it takes. All I'm trying do to is get to a place where somebody else has to make the decision."

Jim added that he had seen one very positive sign: Carmelo Martinez, a power hitter, had tried to bunt before he struck out. "That could be a plus for me. I think Martinez was the Number Three hitter in their lineup. If it's a windy day and he wants to bunt, if they're thinking about my weakness, that can only help me."

Four days later, Jim pitched again in Phoenix, Arizona. This time, his opponents were the mighty Oakland A's, the defending American League champions. The Angels won, 9-4, but Jim struggled a bit during the two innings he pitched. He gave up three walks and a hit and allowed a run to score when he bobbled a ground ball that would have been an easy double play. Jim made up for it by striking out feared slugger Jose Canseco with runners on second and third.

"There were a few butterflies in my stomach out there," Jim said after the game. "I got caught up in who was out there, rather than what I could do."

Once again, Jim received praise from friend and foe alike. "I've been very impressed with him ever since he's been here," said Angels catcher Lance Parrish. "He was trying to overthrow to the first couple of batters he faced. His second inning was much better. He has as live a fastball as I've caught in quite a while. I've caught him several times and he's almost torn the glove off my hand. He throws as hard as anyone in camp."

"He looks legitimate," Jose Canseco said.

"I hope they trade him to the National League," said A's manager Tony LaRussa.

Jim's chances of making the Angels looked brighter every day. "When you see someone with his amount of talent and you admire the person on top of that, it's tough to stay objective," Doug Rader said. "If you're to be perfectly objective about Jim Abbott, then he's certainly one of the 10 best pitchers in our organization. And if he's one of the 10 best we have, how can he not make our pitching staff?"

Jim's spectacular spring increased the attention he received. A small army of reporters and photographers followed wherever he went, and a Japanese camera crew filmed him. Jim got so tired of doing interviews that the Angels told reporters that he would not be speaking to them for two days.

"I felt like I was giving answers from a notebook," Jim

said. "Anyone would get tired being asked the same questions. I try to handle it the best I can. It's a lot of attention. Some of it's nice. I think it's an acknowledgement that there is some talent there. If I wasn't doing well and I wasn't at this level, then me being born with one hand wouldn't matter. But at the same time, if I had two hands, there wouldn't be all this attention. I'd just be another left-handed pitcher."

Tim Mead, the Angels publicity director, did his best to portray Jim that way. Mead decided to take any mention of a handicap out of Jim's biography in the team's media guide. "There's no need for it," he said.

Tom Treblehorn, the manager of the Milwaukee Brewers, agreed after his team faced Jim for the first time. "The only handicap I see is the hitters who have to face him," he said.

Jim received a tremendous amount of fan mail that spring. One day, a reporter noticed that Jim's locker was crammed with more than 100 letters and asked, "One week's fan mail?"

"That's just today's," Jim replied.

Jim worried that he was receiving so much attention

while his teammates were being ignored. He didn't have to worry, though. His teammates understood and they tried to make him feel like part of the team. They kidded him by saying, "Hey, you've only got one hand!" The only thing they didn't like was facing him in intra-squad games.

"You always know which field he's throwing on," Doug Rader said. "Nothing happens. He shuts it down."

Jim shut down the Milwaukee Brewers in his third outing. He threw fastballs, hard sliders, and slow curves that fooled Brewer hitters Jim Gantner, Greg Brock, and Glenn Braggs.

"I felt more comfortable," Jim said later. "That was the best stuff I've had all spring. I took my time and it helped. Just the novelty of being in big league surroundings is starting to wear off. My confidence is starting to rise to the level where I think I can compete with these guys."

That was obvious to Angels pitching coach Marcel Lachemann. "We don't want him to get into a situation that's over his head, but Jim has excelled all his life," he said. "He is very mature for his age, a classy young man. He has a very solid delivery. There's very little we can teach him."

The only problem was that the Angels already had five

good starting pitchers: Mike Witt, Bert Blyleven, Dan Petry, Kirk McCaskill, and Chuck Finley. The only place left for Jim was in the bullpen and manager Doug Rader hesitated about making Jim a relief pitcher. "We'd need a problem with one of our five starters," he said. "Jim's a starter. We're not thinking of him as a relief pitcher."

Rader also suspected that Jim would give him no choice but to put him in the starting rotation. "I wouldn't put any restraints on where Jim might pitch this year," he said. "To categorize him would be unfair. He's a unique human being."

The suspense surrounding Jim continued to build as the end of spring training approached. Yet Jim wasn't worried. "The toughest part, honestly, is the media," he said. "You're trying to get acquainted with a new team, new guys, and there's constantly someone with a camera in front of you, telling you you're different, singling you out at a time when you want to be as inconspicuous as you can."

Jim became more conspicuous after Dan Petry developed a sore shoulder in late March. Doug Rader knew that if Petry did not recover quickly, he might have to add Jim to the starting rotation. "We've got to look at this very

79

carefully," he said. "Jim has got to fit in there somewhere. The thing about Abbott that sticks in my mind is that whenever he goes out there, you think something good is going to happen. You think you're going to win. Not many people have that kind of presence."

Jim felt bad that his good fortune had come at Petry's expense. As a kid, Jim had rooted for the Detroit Tigers when Petry had been one of their star pitchers. "I was always a big fan of his," Jim said. "He and Jack Morris. They were the top 1-2 combination in the league. I tried to emulate him. I've watched how hard he works. Since coming here, I've seen how nice a guy he is. Whether I'm a starter or a reliever here, I hope it's because I do well. I'd hate to make a team just because somebody got hurt."

Before long, there were reports in newspapers that Jim and Petry had become rivals. Petry denied it was true. "That's something you guys have created a little bit," he told reporters. "Him being the eye-opener and the darling and that kind of stuff. That kind of puts me in an uncomfortable situation. I mean, nobody's rooting against me, but he's the interesting story. It should be that he's going to make the team because of his stuff not because of my shoulder or that it's good for the media for him to be here. If there's some-body better than me, then they deserve to be here, but I don't root against him. That's awful."

A week or so before Opening Day, Doug Rader took a look at Jim's spring training statistics: 2 wins, 1 loss, a 5.29 ERA, 12 strikeouts, and only 4 walks in a total of 17 innings pitched. Then he made a decision. Jim was on the team! He had become only the 15th player since 1965 to join a major league team without ever playing in the minors.

"There's been only two balls hit hard off of him," Rader said. "You have to keep in mind that's not your normal twenty-one-year-old we're talking about here. The quality of effort, his stuff, his composure, his whole program is not comparable to any other twenty-one-year-old I've ever been around."

Jim was extremely happy, but he was also more deter-mined than ever to make the most of the tremendous oppor-tunity he had been given. "I'd be lying to you if I said I didn't feel pressure to justify the decision to keep me," he said. "The last thing I want to hear in three weeks is 'He was here too early.' But I don't think that's going to be the case. I feel like I deserve to be here."

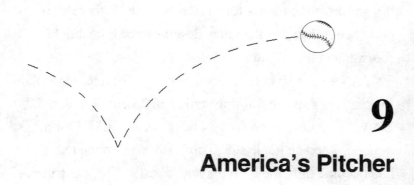

9

America's Pitcher

When Jim walked into the Angels clubhouse in Anaheim Stadium for the first time just before Opening Day of the 1989 season, the clubhouse boy handed him a telegram. It read: "Congratulations. Looking forward to seeing you pitch this year." The telegram was signed by Nolan Ryan, the great pitcher for the Texas Rangers who has struck out more batters (more than 5,000) and thrown more no-hitters (6) than any other pitcher in major league history.

Jim was stunned. At first, he thought it was a joke and he suspected that Bert Blyleven, the team's prankster, had sent it. But when his teammates passed the telegram around as if it had been sent by God, Jim knew it was real.

The Angels opened the 1989 season with a 9-2 loss to Chicago at Anaheim. Jim was not scheduled to pitch until the fifth game, against the Seattle Mariners, but reporters were already following him. Four TV crews from Japan were among the media army that stalked his every move. The Japanese asked many questions, such as:

How did it feel to strike out the great hitter, Jose Canseco?

What will be the first ball you throw against Seattle?

"They also asked me what my blood type was," Jim says. "That might be the strangest one yet. They asked me a lot of questions about spirit and determination and the inner kinds of things. They seem to be amazed by what I do, thinking that I have some special drive. They look at boxer Mike Tyson or sprinter Carl Lewis the same way. I think the special kind of determination in all athletes is something that's looked up to over there."

Jim made his major league debut on Saturday night, April 8, 1989, at Anaheim Stadium. A crowd of 46,847 fans cheered Jim on as his parents and brother watched from seats in a private box. Three times as many reporters than usual were there, too. The newspaper, *Baseball America,* called the game, "The second most spectacular debut in major league history behind Jackie Robinson." In 1947, Robinson became the first black player in major league history when he joined the Brooklyn Dodgers.

Jim tried his best to ignore all the excitement and concentrate on pitching well. "Hopefully, things will go well, but if they don't, it won't be the end of the world," Jim said before the game.

Unfortunately, things did not go as he had hoped. Harold Reynolds of the Mariners led off the game with a hard single to rightfield. Henry Cotto followed with a single that sent Reynolds to third. Jim then threw a wild pitch and Cotto raced to second. Both runners scored on groundouts and the Angels were quickly behind, 2-0.

Jim settled down and pitched into the fifth inning, but when the Mariners scored four more runs, he was taken out of the game. The crowd gave Jim a standing ovation as he left the field, but the Angels ended up losing, 7-0.

After the game, a special press conference was held. A large crowd of reporters gathered around as Jim stood at a podium and answered questions. His parents watched from the back of the room. "I can't believe this is what the poor guy has had to go through every time," Doug Rader said.

Jim was asked how he felt about his first major league game. He replied that he felt bad about letting his teammates down. "Overall, I'm a little disappointed," he said. "It's hard right now to look at this day in a real positive light. I didn't throw real well and that took some of the sweetness out of it. I will look at things more objectively tomorrow and build on this for the next time. And in a few years, maybe I'll look back and say, 'It wasn't so bad.'"

Doug Rader said, "I'm sure he was churning inside, but he held it in."

Jim was asked if he had been nervous. "Maybe when I was warming up," he replied. "I was caught up in the hoopla. The crowd support was a big deal for me, but then it was just another game. After the first couple of batters got hits, I knew I was in a battle. I learned at this level, you can't just throw the ball over the plate and you have to concentrate on every pitch. My mind was not as clearly focused as I would want."

Jim's mom said that she was the most nervous of all. "I kept saying, 'If we could just get through three innings,'" she said. "Then after that happened, I said, 'Now if we can get through six more.'"

Mr. Abbott told reporters that the standing ovation Jim received as he left the mound was the highlight of the evening. "That was really nice," he said. "Support and encouragement like that lets you go back out there and give it another try."

Over in Seattle's clubhouse, Mariners manager Jim Lefebvre [*Leh-FEE-ver*] said Jim had not pitched as poorly as it seemed. "He was around the plate all night," he said. "I liked him. I think he can pitch at the big league level."

Doug Rader agreed. "I don't think he'll ever have another outing like this," he said. "Under the circumstances, he was outstanding. He showed no outward signs of losing his composure. I'm proud of him. Hopefully, the amount of attention he's getting will come now from the fact that he deserves it and not from the other things."

Of course, "the other things" that Doug Rader was referring to were Jim's handicap and the fact that he had made the major leagues in spite of it. Reporters did not stop talking and writing about them. Some again accused the Angels of letting Jim pitch only as a publicity stunt. That accusation made Doug Rader extremely upset.

"Do you have the guts to sit there and tell me he has a handicap?" Rader yelled at a group of reporters one day early in the season. "Do you? Well, he doesn't. He's the least handicapped person I know. To me, all that talk of a publicity stunt is incredibly distasteful. He could have pitched a perfect game and it wouldn't have been different. He'll still have to prove himself."

Jim handled the accusation more calmly. "I can see where it would be an argument, but I would hope that maybe I'm proving them wrong," he said. "As long as there are questions in people's minds, that will be around. I think it's going to take maybe a year of performing at a respectable level here. If we start winning and every fifth day I'm out there pitching, people will start saying, 'Hey, he's helping the team. That's no publicity stunt.'"

Jim's roommate, Rick Turner, defended him by saying, "If that was the case, then we'd also have a 50-year-old pitcher, a 17-year-old, and a guy who's three-feet-tall on the team."

Jim's first few weeks with the Angels were frustrating. He lost his second start, 5-0, to the Oakland A's. Then his third start was postponed because of cold weather. Jim also caught the flu and was unable to pitch for 11 days. All the while, reporters kept making a big deal about his handicap and some doubted that he was good enough to succeed in the big leagues. Jim began to let these things bother him.

"Right now, I'm just trying to be a baseball player and trying to make my way onto this team for good and to do well," he said. "The other things that people are asking me don't have anything to do with baseball. I don't know if that's always fair to ask of me. I want things to settle down. I've found a place to live, so things can be normal again. I want to get settled in and let my teammates know they can count on me. I feel like I've earned a spot on the team. I feel like I belong and so do the Angels."

On April 24, Jim beat the Baltimore Orioles, 3-2, for his first major league victory. The Orioles had runners in scoring position in each of the first three innings, but Jim hung tough. He pitched six innings and gave up only four hits and two runs. He then went to the trainer's room to put an ice pack on his arm. He watched the game on TV and saw relief pitcher Bryan Harvey get out of a jam with the bases loaded and two outs in the eighth inning. Harvey fell behind pinch-hitter Jim Traber, three balls and one strike, and was close to walking in the tying run. But he battled back to strike out Traber and end the inning.

"When Harv got Traber, I jumped up with my arms waving," Jim said. "I guess it's a good thing I wasn't in the dugout for that. I'd have been jumping up and screaming."

"Jim's knees had to be shaking with the bases juiced there," Harvey said. "He'd pitched his heart out and I'm glad we won."

"I'm glad I didn't have to hit against him," said Orioles manager Frank Robinson. "He looked very good. He had an excellent slider and kept the ball inside on the right-handed hitters."

Orioles outfielder Phil Bradley said, "He's got three good pitches and his fastball has enough velocity that you have to honor it. We really didn't get too many good swings off him and that's the sign of a good pitcher."

Bradley's teammate, designated hitter Larry Sheets, told reporters that it had been hard to tell that Jim is handicapped. "It just doesn't cross your mind when you get to home plate," he said. "He has the hand that counts and he's going to win some games. I was impressed. He has real good composure and he can throw four pitches over the plate at any time in the count. He threw me a big old curveball. . . and I wasn't looking for that."

The victory ended a three-game losing streak for the Angels and made Jim the first left-handed rookie starter to win a game for California since 1981. It was also a big relief.

"I didn't feel like I was earning my keep," Jim said after the game. "I felt like I was coming to the park and getting a free ride. Sometimes you begin to feel like you don't belong. That's why this win is very special. Now I feel more and more a member of the Angels."

Jim had felt awkward around his teammates, but after Bert Blyleven set Jim's shoes on fire during a crowded press conference, he realized he was one of the guys. His teammates liked him and they often got a kick out of his enthusiasm. They kidded him whenever he got excited during games. One day during a game in Oakland, California, Jim said to himself, "Today, no rookie mistakes. I'm not giving them any reason to get on me." But during the game, Jim spotted a fight in the stands. Apparently without thinking, he jumped off the bench and yelled, "Fight! Fight!" One of his teammates then poked him in the ribs and said, "Uh, we don't do that up here in the majors."

Jim sat down red-faced with embarrassment.

After the game against Baltimore, Jim went out on the town with Orioles pitcher Gregg Olson, who had been his teammate during the 1987 Pan Am Games. "Jim's the greatest," Olson said. "He's an amazing guy. People have no idea what pressure he has had. There were the Olympics, there was the draft, there was his handicap, there was his making the major leagues. For his sake, I was hoping he wouldn't make it so he wouldn't have the pressure right away. But now I'm glad he's here."

So were the Angels, who won 16 of their next 20 games to move into a tie for first place in the American League's Western Division. Jim won two games during that streak. The second was against ace pitcher Roger Clemens of the Boston Red Sox on May 17 in Anaheim.

"I'm excited about it," Jim said before the game. "I've always watched him and obviously he's a great pitcher. I think it will be kind of a thrill to pitch against him and I'm looking forward to it."

Jim allowed only four hits and no runs in nine innings as the Angels beat Clemens and the Red Sox, 5-0. When Jim went into the clubhouse after the game, he saw that his teammates had made a white carpet of towels that stretched from the door to his locker.

Jim's victory over Boston convinced many people that he belonged in the majors. He was soon cheered in every stadium he visited and bumper stickers calling him "America's Pitcher" appeared in Anaheim. Groups of handi-capped children went to Anaheim Stadium whenever he pitched and he received a shopping cart full of fan mail each week. National magazines such as *Time, Newsweek, Sports Illustrated, Sports Illustrated For Kids,* and *Life* did feature stories about him. So did a Japanese sports magazine that featured pictures of Jim sitting on the bench, pitching, and even standing next to a cactus in Arizona with a big smile on his face.

"Aren't these pictures hilarious?" Jim asked a reporter one day. "I can't explain the fascination."

By midseason, Jim felt much more at home in Southern California. One day, a couple of his high school friends came out to visit and they spent an afternoon driving through Hollywood. Jim decided then that he really liked his new home. He had also adjusted to the constant travel that is part of life in the major leagues. For that, he credited his experiences with Team USA during the summer of 1988.

"I think it helped mature me," he said. "This year, I've been away from home for a long time, but I'm not real lonely. It's not like it was last year, when I wanted to go home so badly. I can now appreciate what it's like to be 8,000 miles away with three weeks to go before you can come back home."

On July 3, Jim beat the Texas Rangers 5-2. It was his seventh win of the season and it set a record for most wins in one season by a rookie pitcher who had not spent any time in the minor leagues. The old record of six wins had been set by Dick Ruthven of the Philadelphia Phillies in 1973. "Now there's one record I really haven't paid any attention to," Jim said after the game.

On July 9, the Old Timers All-Star Game was held at Anaheim Stadium. Many Hall of Fame players were there and many wanted to visit Jim. Pitcher Warren Spahn stopped by Jim's locker to say hello and second baseman Bobby Doerr brought a baseball for him to sign. Shortstop Ernie Banks asked if he could have his picture taken with Jim. "This is incredible," Jim said.

So was Jim's first season in the major leagues. His final record was 12 wins and 12 losses with a 3.92 earned run average as the Angels finished in third place with 91 wins and 71 losses. Jim had become the first left-handed rookie pitcher to win 10 or more games for the Angels since 1974. He allowed three earned runs or less in a game 21 times and threw two shutouts.

"I felt good about the season," he says. "There were certainly things I'd like to improve upon. But if I compared the last day with the first day, it was an unbelievable improvement."

Most important, Jim made it clear that it did not matter if he had one hand or two. He made only three errors and proved that he has the talent to be a successful major league pitcher.

Perhaps Tim Mead, the Angels publicity director, said it best. One afternoon during the season, Mead answered the telephone in the Angels clubhouse and spoke to a man who said that he had invented an artificial hand designed especially for Jim. Mead listened to the man talk about the hand and then said, "We appreciate your intention, but Jim Abbott has everything he needs."

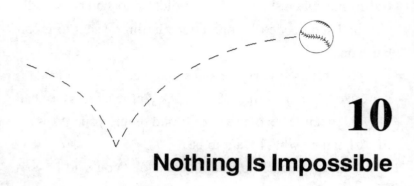

10

Nothing Is Impossible

People admire Jim Abbott because he always seems to do the impossible. "People think of me as an underdog, I guess," he says. "I never have. I always thought of myself as a ballplayer."

It is important to understand that all the remarkable things that Jim has accomplished in his life were impossible only in the minds of other people. This is something he tells everyone, especially the handicapped kids he often visits and writes to.

For example, in June of 1989, a 7-year-old girl named Laura Small sent Jim a letter. She explained how she had been attacked by a mountain lion near San Juan Capistrano,

California, when she was 5 years old. Laura had been badly hurt and she needed 13 operations in three years to repair her wounds.

"I can't use my right hand and most of my right side is paralyzed," Laura wrote. "So, I think you're a great baseball player. I want to become a doctor, and seeing you makes me think I can be what I want to be."

Jim wrote back to Laura and said, "You said in your letter you'd like to become a doctor. If you believe that now and work on it in years to come, there's no reason you can't. I wanted to play baseball when I was growing up. The only people who may have doubted that possibility were those who couldn't accept that my handicap was not a hindrance. Remember, our handicaps are only problems in the eyes of others."

Laura began taking ballet classes and can participate in almost all her gym classes at school. She can even hit a whiffleball one-handed! Yet some of Laura's classmates tease her and, like Jim, she hates being told she is different or special.

"I'm so tired of being special!" Laura told reporter Eric Lichtblau of *The Los Angeles Times*. "I just want to be ordinary! It's like Jim said, you're not really handicapped but people think you are."

Jim knows exactly how Laura feels. "If I have anything to say, it's please don't be discouraging to people," he says. "Always be encouraging and helpful. If anybody had told me I couldn't do it, I wouldn't be here today. But everybody's been so encouraging, so supportive. The reason I'm here is because people gave me a chance. I always loved sports. I could always throw and I had success in baseball. Me and this game, that's all I ever wanted."

Jim is quick to thank and give credit to the many people who have helped him along the way. "Dealing with the adjustments to the major leagues while dealing with the attention has been easier because the players, managers, and coaches accepted me as one of the guys from the outset," he says. "My mom and dad were great. My high school and summer coaches helped me a lot. As much as me, they never took no for an answer. They refused to look at me as being handicapped. I just hope that everyone, not only physically disabled people but people who play baseball but aren't as talented as the next guy, can battle along and keep going and have such a great opportunity as I have now."

Jim's refusal to give in to his handicap is the main reason why he has been able to make the most of his opportunities. He has won much more than awards and games. He has won the respect of his teammates and his opponents.

"I respect Jim for reaching a goal that he set out to accomplish," says pitcher Roger Clemens of the Boston Red Sox. "He's a coach's dream because he goes out and gives 100 percent when there are other guys that have a world of ability that just don't care and don't give 100 percent effort."

Doug Rader says, "You know what the hardest part of talking about Jim is? Everything sounds so cornball. But you know what? It's all true. I love this kid. You can't believe what he's gone through to get here. But he belongs here. He's an amazing person. Once I got to know him, once I found out what type of kid he was, I knew we had to keep him."

Jim has definitely proved that he has the talent to pitch in the major leagues. However, more challenges lie ahead of him. Pitching in the big leagues is a learning process that does not end until a pitcher's career is over. He must learn the strengths and weaknesses of every hitter he faces and frequently change the pitches he throws so they will never know what to expect.

Jim also has some steep odds against him. Ten pitchers since 1965 have begun their major league careers without playing in the minors. Only one, Burt Hooton, who pitched for the Cubs, Dodgers, and Rangers from 1971 to 1985, had a winning record. Others, such as David Clyde, who pitched for the Rangers, and Mike Morgan, who is now with the Dodgers, were not ready to pitch in the majors and their confidence was nearly destroyed.

"I learned how to lose right out of high school," says Morgan, a young pitcher who lost the first nine games he pitched for the Oakland A's in 1978. "I was 18 years old and it killed me. It didn't kill me as a person, but it killed my career."

Many scouts believe that Jim has enough talent to succeed in the big leagues. His chances of doing so are even better now that much of the fuss about his handicap has lessened.

"There's a little less attention and it's kind of nice," Jim says. "I can go out there and be a little bit more focused on the job at hand instead of telling my life story. That's the most difficult thing. You can't do all the interviews and I feel bad about that. That's been the hardest adjustment."

"The amount of distraction was tremendous last year and it takes a lot of energy to deal with that on a day-in, day-out basis," Doug Rader says. "I think a lot of that is past for Jim. He can concentrate on his pitching, probably better than he's ever been able to in the past."

Angels pitcher Bert Blyleven agrees. "I just feel he's going to be stronger this year because he can pitch from day one rather than from the middle of the season. All the pressure is off Jim," he says. "He's demonstrated he can do the job."

Like many major league pitchers, Jim struggled during the first half of the 1990 season. By the All-Star break in early July, his record was only 5-7 and his ERA was 4.74, but Jim did not have much time to prepare for the season. Because of a contract dispute, the owners of the major league teams locked the players out of spring training for several weeks in February and March. Pitchers had less time to strengthen their arms and even stars like Dwight Gooden of the Mets and Mike Scott of the Astros did not begin to pitch well until the middle of the season. Since the All-Star break,

Jim has improved, finishing the season with a 10-14 record and a 4.51 ERA.

It's a safe bet that Jim Abbott will have a successful major league career no matter what challenge he faces. The reason is simple: Jim believes in himself.

"When it comes down to it, I'll take my ability with anyone else's," he says. "I'm comfortable how I am. I don't need to be like everyone else to be happy. The day I'm judged just on how I pitch is what I am striving for."

Baseball Field

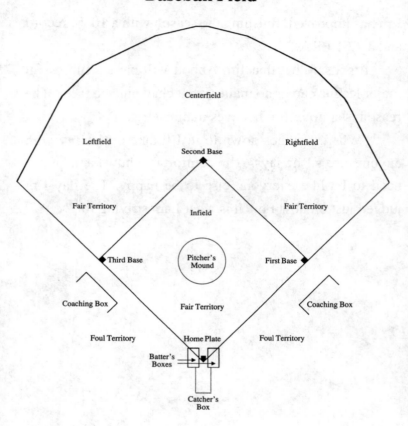

Jim's Major League Statistics

1989

Won-Lost	ERA	Innings Pitched	Earned Runs	Strikeouts
12-12	3.92	181.1	79	115

1990

Won-Lost	ERA	Innings Pitched	Earned Runs	Strikeouts
10-14	4.51	211.2	106	105

A Letter from Jim Abbott

One morning in April 1989, a 5-year-old girl named Erin Bower went shopping with her mother in the town of Castleton Farms, Indiana. While they were in a store, Erin noticed a tube of toothpaste on a counter. When she picked it up, it exploded. Some cruel, sick person had put an explosive in the tube.

Erin wasn't killed, but she lost her left hand in the blast. People all around the country heard about it on the news and many of them sent letters of sympathy to the little girl. One of the letters was from Jim. Here's what it said:

Dear Erin:

Perhaps somewhere later in your lifetime you will properly understand this letter and the feelings that go behind it. Regardless, I wanted to send something along now after being made aware of your terrible accident.

As your parents have probably told you, I was born without a right hand. That automatically made me different from the other kids I was around. But you know what? It made me different only in their eyes. You see, I figured that's what the good Lord wanted me to work with. So it was my responsibility to become as good as I could at whatever I chose to do, regardless of my handicap.

I just won my first major league game. When the final out was made, a lot of things went through my mind. I thought of my parents and all the help they provided; my brother and his support; and all of my friends along the way. The only thing, Erin, that I didn't pay attention to was my handicap. You see, it had nothing to do with anything.

You're a young lady now with a tremendous life ahead of you. Whether you want to be an athlete, a doctor, a lawyer, or anything else, it will be up to you, and only you, how far you go. Certainly there will be some tough times ahead, but with dedication and love of life, you'll be successful in any field you choose. I'll look forward to reading about you in the future.

Again, my best,

Jim Abbott, California Angels.

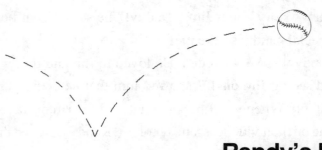

Randy's Hero

Randy Sobek was born in San Diego, California, in 1982. He was only 3 days old when doctors removed four fingers and part of the thumb on his left hand because the hand had been badly damaged at birth.

Randy spent the first three weeks of his life in the hospital. He later needed nine operations on his hand, but he was still handicapped. Mr. and Mrs. Sobek were unsure how to raise their son, but their doctor told them, "Randy will become how you treat him."

Like Mr. and Mrs. Abbott, Carol and Duke Sobek treated their son like a normal child and encouraged him to play sports.

One day in 1987, Randy was watching TV when he saw a news story about Jim. "Daddy!" he said. "That boy has a special hand just like me!"

Randy was very excited. He loved to run and throw a ball and seeing Jim on TV showed him that he could play baseball too. Whenever Jim pitched, Randy's parents taped the game on their videocassette recorder. Randy watched the tapes constantly.

"I was happy because he has a special hand, too, " Randy says. "I want to field just like he does when I play baseball or tee-ball. I practice with my daddy a lot."

And just like Jim, Randy was given an artificial arm before he started kindergarten. However, some kids were frightened by it. So Randy and his mom spoke to the class.

"We explained in detail why Randy has the hand and how it works," his mom says. "We passed the hand around and let everyone see it. One mother came up to me the next day and thanked me. She said her little girl had been afraid of Randy, but now he was her hero."

You can probably guess who Randy's hero is.

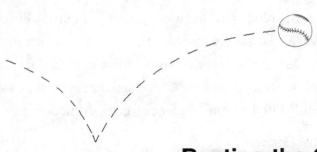

Beating the Odds

Jim is one of many physically challenged athletes who have played in the major leagues. Here are some of the others:

Gene Bearden

He was seriously injured when his ship was hit by a torpedo during World War II. Aluminum plates were placed in his head and knee and he spent two years in the hospital. Bearden later recovered to pitch in the major leagues from 1947 to 1953. His best year was 1948, when he won 20 games for the Cleveland Indians.

Lew Brissie

Like Bearden, Brissie was seriously injured during World War II. He nearly lost his left leg, but was later able to play while wearing a heavy brace. Brissie pitched for the Philadelphia Athletics and the Cleveland Indians from 1947 to 1953. In 1949, he won 16 games for the Athletics.

Mordecai Brown

He lost two fingers on his right hand in an accident when he was 7 years old. Still able to grip and throw a baseball, he pitched for the St. Louis Cardinals, the Chicago Cubs, and the Cincinnati Reds from 1903 to 1916. Brown won 208 games during his major league career, including 20 or more six seasons in a row. He was elected to the Baseball Hall of Fame in 1949.

Hugh Daily

As a teenager in the 1870s, Daily lost the lower part of his right arm when fireworks accidentally exploded near him. In that era, baseball players did not use fielder's gloves, so when he played Daily placed a pad on the stump of his arm and learned to knock batted balls into the air and catch them on the way down. Daily later pitched in the National League from 1882 to 1887, and won 73 games during his career. In 1884, he struck out 483 batters and pitched four one-hitters!

Bud Daley

Like Jim Abbott, Daley was born with a handicapped right arm. He learned to throw, hit, and field so well that he later spent 10 years in the big leagues with the Cleveland Indians, Kansas City A's, and New York Yankees. He won 16 games for the A's in both 1959 and 1960.

Jim Eisenreich

An outfielder who is currently playing for the Kansas City Royals, Eisenreich overcame a serious nervous disorder. Whenever he was on the field, he would begin to twitch and get dizzy. The disorder was so bad that Eisenreich quit the major leagues in 1984. Two years later, he returned and, in 1989, he batted .293 for the Royals.

Pete Gray

After his right arm was crushed in the spokes of a wheel when he was 6 years old, Gray learned to hit by tossing rocks in the air and swatting them with a bat when they came down. He later became the minor league Southern Association's Most Valuable Player in 1944 by batting .333 with 68 stolen bases. The next year, Gray played 77 games as an outfielder for the St. Louis Browns but batted only .218. A movie about Gray's life, *A Winner Never Quits*, was made in 1986.

Chick Hafey

An outfielder with the St. Louis Cardinals and the Cincinnati Reds from 1924 to 1937, Hafey's eyesight was so poor that he needed eyeglasses with very thick lenses. Hafey actually had trouble reading signs on the roadside or in train stations, but hitting a baseball wasn't a problem for him. Hafey's career batting average was .317! He was elected to the Baseball Hall of Fame in 1971.

William Hoy

Hoy, who was totally deaf, was a fine major league outfielder from 1888 to 1902. He had a career batting average of .288, and he even set a record by throwing three runners out at home plate in one game.

Barney Mussill

A left-handed relief pitcher, Mussill was left almost blind by an explosion during World War II. He spent three months recovering in the hospital and he later appeared in 16 games for the Philadelphia Phillies in 1944.

Dick Sipek

Another player who overcame deafness to reach the big leagues, Sipek was introduced to baseball by Luther Taylor. Taylor was a teacher at the Illinois School of the Deaf and Sipek was a student. In 1945, Sipek played 82 games as an outfielder with the Cincinnati Reds and batted .244.

Walter Stewart

After he lost a finger on his right hand in an accident, Stewart learned to pitch as a lefty. He went on to win 100 games for the Detroit Tigers, St. Louis Browns, Washington Senators, and Cleveland Indians from 1921 to 1935.

Tom Sunkel

A left-handed pitcher, Sunkel lost the sight in his left eye because of a childhood accident with a popgun. He later spent six seasons in the major leagues with the St. Louis Cardinals, New York Giants, and Brooklyn Dodgers from 1937 to 1944.

Luther Taylor

Like Hoy, Taylor was deaf. He pitched for the New York Giants and the Cleveland Indians from 1900 to 1908. It is believed that Taylor was the reason that umpires began to use hand signals when they call balls and strikes. Taylor's best year was 1904, when he won 21 games for the Giants. That season, his teammates in New York's starting rotation were Hall of Fame pitchers Christy Mathewson and Iron Man McGinnity. The Giants, by the way, won the National League pennant that year!

Where Are They Now?

Jim Abbott was one of 23 players on the 1988 U.S. Baseball Team that won the gold medal at the Summer Olympics in Seoul, South Korea. Like Jim, each of his teammates was drafted by a major league team. Here is a list of some of those players and where they have been playing:

Bret Barberie: Shortstop

Bret Barberie was chosen in the seventh round of the 1988 draft by the Montreal Expos. He played second base for Montreal's Double A team in Jacksonville, Florida, during the 1990 season.

Andy Benes: Pitcher

Andy was the first player chosen in the 1988 draft of amateur players. He made his major league debut in 1989 with the San Diego Padres, winning six games and losing three. In 1990, Andy was 10-11 with a 3.60 ERA for San Diego.

Jeff Branson: Shortstop

Jeff also spent the 1990 season playing second base for a Double A team, the Chattanooga (Tennessee) Lookouts of the Cincinnati Reds organization. Jeff was the Reds' first draft choice in 1988.

Pat Combs: Pitcher

Pat was chosen in the first round of the 1988 draft by the Philadelphia Phillies. He made his major league debut in 1989, winning four and losing none with a 2.09 ERA. In 1989, Pat won 10 and lost 10 for Philadelphia.

Mike Fiore: Outfielder

Mike Fiore spent the 1990 season with an A League team in Florida. His team, the St. Petersburg Cardinals, is part of the St. Louis Cardinals' organization. The Cards drafted Mike in the fifth round of the 1988 draft.

Tom Goodwin: Outfielder
The Los Angeles Dodgers chose Tom Goodwin in the first round of the 1989 draft. He spent the 1990 season playing for their Double A team in San Antonio, Texas.

Ty Griffin: Second Baseman
Ty Griffin was chosen in the first round of the 1988 draft by the Chicago Cubs. He spent the 1990 season with their Double A team in Charlotte, North Carolina, where he has been learning to play third base.

Billy Maase: Outfielder
Billy Maase played for the New York Yankees' A League team in Fort Lauderdale, Florida, in 1990. Billy was drafted by New York in the seventh round of the 1988 draft.

Tino Martinez: First Baseman
The Seattle Mariners drafted Tino Martinez in the first round of the 1988 draft, and he played for the Mariners Double A minor league team in Williamsport, Pennsylvania. In 1990 he was promoted to their Triple A club in Calgary, Canada, and batted over .300 before joining the Mariners late in the season. He batted .211 in 21 games for Seattle.

Ben McDonald: Pitcher

Ben was the first player chosen in the 1989 amateur draft. He pitched in only two minor league games that year before joining the Baltimore Orioles in late September and winning his only start. An injury in spring training slowed Ben a bit in 1990, but he recovered to win 10 and lose 14 for the Orioles that season.

Mike Milchin: Pitcher

Mike Milchin was also drafted by the Cardinals. He was chosen in the second round of the 1989 draft and spent the 1990 season with St. Louis' Double A team, the Arkansas Travelers.

Mickey Morandini: Infielder

In 1988, the Philadelphia Phillies made infielder Mickey Morandini a fifth-round draft choice. He made his major league debut with the Phillies in the 1990 season and batted .183 in 23 games. He is expected to be their starting second baseman in 1991.

Charles Nagy: Pitcher

Charles Nagy was drafted by the Cleveland Indians in the 17th round of the 1988 draft. In 1990, he jumped to the majors from Cleveland's Double A team in Canton-Akron, Ohio, after he won 8 and lost 4 with a fine 2.83 ERA. With the Indians, Charles had a record of 2-4.

Doug Robbins: Catcher

The Baltimore Orioles drafted Doug Robbins in the 10th round in 1988. He spent the 1990 season with Baltimore's Double A team in Hagerstown, Maryland.

Scott Servais: Catcher

Scott Servais was chosen by the Houston Astros in the third round of the 1988 draft. He spent the season playing for Houston's Triple A team in Tucson, Arizona.

Dave Silvestri: Shortstop

Dave Silvestri was drafted by the Houston Astros in the second round of the 1988 draft. Houston traded Dave to the New York Yankees during the 1990 season and he played for New York's A league team in Prince William, Virginia.

Joe Slusarski: Pitcher

Joe Slusarski was drafted by the Oakland A's in the second round of the 1988 draft. He pitched for their Double A team in Huntsville, Alabama, in 1990.

Ed Sprague: Third Baseman

Another first round pick in the 1988 draft, Ed Sprague joined the Toronto Blue Jays' organization. In 1990, Ed played for Toronto's Triple A team in Syracuse, New York.

Robin Ventura: Third Baseman

Robin Ventura was also a first round draft pick in 1988. He joined the Chicago White Sox late in the 1989 season and played in only 16 games. In 1990, Robin spent the entire season with the White Sox, batting .252 with five homers and 53 RBIs.

Ted Wood: Outfielder

The San Francisco Giants made Ted Wood a first round draft choice in 1988. He played for their Double A team in Shreveport, Louisiana, during the 1990 season.

Glossary
Baseball Terms

All-Star Game: The annual game played between the best players in the National League and the American League. The make-up of each team is based on votes cast by sportswriters, coaches, players, and fans.

Balk: An illegal move made by a pitcher having to do with his pitching motion, including failing to complete the motion once started. Each base runner advances one base.

Ball: A pitch thrown outside the strike zone.

Base on Balls: Also known as a walk. When the batter advances to first base because four pitches thrown during his at-bat were outside the strike zone.

Bullpen: An area outside the playing field where pitchers warm up during a game.

Bunt: A soft hit that results from the batter holding the bat out and letting the ball hit it, rather than swinging the bat at the ball.

Earned Run: A run that is scored without an error having been made by the team on the field.

Earned Run Average: Also called an ERA. The average number of earned runs per game scored against a pitcher. An ERA is determined by dividing the total number of earned runs by the total number of innings pitched and multiplying by nine.

Error: A fielding misplay or wild throw that allows the batter to reach base or a runner to advance.

Full Count: When a pitcher has thrown three balls and two strikes to a single batter. It is called a full count because the next pitch will be the last one.

Hits:
- **Single** – A base hit that allows a batter to reach first base.
- **Double** – A base hit that allows a batter to reach second base.
- **Triple** – A base hit that allows a batter to reach third base.
- **Home Run** – A hit by a player that allows him to round the bases and score a run. Home runs are usually hit over the fence in the outfield.

Minor League: A training league system by which most players get to the major leagues. Each major league club has its own minor league system (also called farm system). There are four levels in the minor leagues — rookie, A, Double A, and Triple A. The largest number of players are in the rookie league or in the A League. As they get better, they move up through the system closer to the major leagues.

Pickoff: When a pitcher tries to throw out a base runner who has taken a big lead off any of the bases.

Pitcher: The player who starts the action by throwing the ball to the catcher.